Profiles in Colonial History

Solitude Press

Profiles in Colonial History

Copyright © 2008 Aleck Loker

ISBN-13   978-1-928874-16-4

Printed in the United States of America

Published by:

Solitude Press
212 Brooks Street
Williamsburg VA 23185

To the Williamsburg Writers Group
for their support, patience, and editorial advice.

And to Ann
for her love and unfailing encouragement.

Contents

Forward

From the first English settlement attempts in North America through the American Revolution, many brave men and women contributed to the foundations of the United States during the colonial period. *Profiles in Colonial History* presents the lives and contributions of six individuals—five men and one woman—who risked their lives and fortunes to ensure the continuation of the American adventure.

Although these six people lived in different times during the two-hundred year colonial period, they shared certain personal characteristics that set them apart. They were inquisitive, social or political pioneers, and not content with the status quo.

They also shared a belief in certain fundamental human rights: equality and freedom. That is not to say their view extended those rights to all people, but, for their time and in their society, they espoused controversial—we would say liberal—ideas regarding human rights.

Some suffered for their beliefs; others avoided public censure. The English Church and government branded Thomas Harriot, the first person profiled in this book, a heretic because of his scientific beliefs; he narrowly escaped execution. Patrick Henry received popular support for his aggressive stance against the crown, but many of his fellow burgesses shunned him as a rabble-rouser. Margaret Brent stood up to rebels and held the Maryland colony together when the governor had fled to Virginia. She also made a dramatic stand for women's rights two-hundred years before the suffrage movement began.

These six colonial figures promoted ideas that were far ahead of their time and in many cases put these advocates at personal risk. Their lives demonstrate the spirit of freedom and independence embodied in the United States. Their stories show that freedom and independence are difficult to achieve, maintain, and balance with concerns of safety and security. These six individuals succeeded in advancing their beliefs at times when others hesitated due to religious, social, or political pressure.

Many other worthy individuals could appear in these profiles, but I have chosen these six—some obscure, others well known—because they each offer a lesson in public service, personal integrity, intellectual curiosity, and the difficulty of achieving success in a world of conflict. All of them navigated between conflicting forces and managed to succeed not only personally but also on behalf of their fellow citizens.

Many people have helped with these biographical sketches. Bob Hill, retail manager with the Colonial Williamsburg Foundation, suggested the idea for these stories. Dr. Lois Green Carr, Staff Historian for Historic St. Mary's City, provided her knowledge and extensive research materials on early Maryland figures such as Margaret Brent. Eileen Alberti, at the Shakespeare Centre Records Office, Shakespeare Birthplace Trust, Stratford-upon-Avon, provided a unique insight into life in Gloucestershire in the late sixteenth and early seventeenth century. Thanks to Richard Schumann for his insight into the life of Patrick Henry. Finally, I want to thank the Williamsburg Writers: John Conlee, Alastair Connell, Kit Fournier, Jug Gerard, Mac Laird, and Sally Stiles. They have consistently encouraged me, have given sound advice, and have exhibited more patience than one should expect. And, I thank Ann for her love and encouragement of whatever I attempt.

Profiles in Colonial History first appeared as a series of individual biographical pamphlets. This volume provides all six stories in a single binding. I hope you find these brief biographies interesting and inspiring.

Aleck Loker
Williamsburg, Virginia

Thomas Harriot
Mathematician, Scientist, Explorer of Virginia

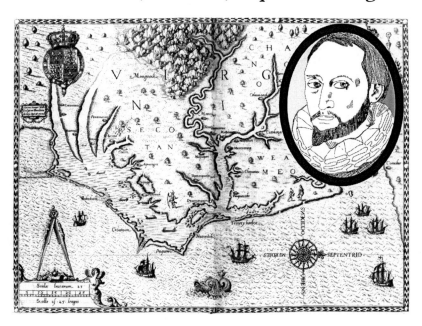

Chapter 1
Thomas Harriot
Mathematician, Scientist, Explorer of Virginia

On June 23, 1585, Thomas Harriot, standing on the port side of the *Tiger*, smelled the sweet aroma of magnolia and honeysuckle carried out to sea on breezes from the west. Manteo and Wanchese, two Indian men, stood alongside. All three strained to glimpse the first sight of that low-lying strip of barrier islands known today as the Outer Banks of North Carolina, the home the two Indians hadn't seen for nine months. Soon they saw the surf rising up and crashing onto the hard, sandy beach, sending plumes of spray into the air. Manteo recognized the island of Croatoan, where his mother was weroansqua, the tribal leader.

Harriot smiled to see how excited Manteo was to be home. He knew that the young Indian couldn't wait to show off his English friend with all of his fascinating and mysterious devices—things none of the other Indians in that part of the world had ever seen. Manteo and Wanchese had traveled to England the previous autumn with the first of Sir Walter Ralegh's expeditions to the New World. They had lived with Thomas Harriot in Ralegh's home, *Durham House*, on the north bank of the Thames River. Harriot had worked hard with them to learn as much of their Algonquian language as time permitted and to teach them English. By the time they arrived in America, all three could converse easily among themselves in either language.

A dedicated teacher, Harriot had led the two Indians through a number of scientific experiments, showing them how a glass lens could concentrate the sun's rays and set tinder alight, demonstrating how a magnet could attract pieces of iron, and showing them how a compass needle always pointed in one direction no matter how you turned the compass. He had also shown them what he called "perspective glasses," today's telescopes. Soon Manteo would lead Harriot and the other Englishmen to Indian villages in the land Ralegh called Virginia; there Harriot would teach the Indians about English science and religion, and they would teach Harriot about the natural wonders of Ossomocommac—as they called their land—and teach him about their society.

Harriot and an Indian with a lens, starting a fire

The explorations, however, started on a bad note. As their Portuguese pilot attempted to steer *Tiger* through an inlet the Indians called Wococon, the ship ran hard aground. The pounding surf slammed the hull repeatedly against the shoals and soon water poured in, spoiling most of their supplies and threatening to sink the ship. Luckily, the tide turned and the *Tiger's* master finally made the ship fast near the shore. There the crew careened the ship and repaired the damaged hull. Once repaired, they managed to get the ship to a safe offshore anchorage. The admiral of the expeditionary fleet, Sir Richard Grenville, stormed about the ship, cursing Simon Fernandez, the pilot, for his stupidity.

Grenville's hot temper couldn't dampen Harriot's excitement or that of his Indian companions. They were about to embark upon the first scientific study of North America ever conducted by the English. The report of the expedition stands to this day as the most useful account of the natural resources and Native American society at the time of first contact, invaluable to a succession of linguists, anthropologists, historians, cartographers, and ecologists. Thomas Harriot's report, illustrated with drawings produced by fellow-explorer John White, first appeared in print in 1588. Although he would have a long, productive life of scientific experimentation, Harriot's account of this expedition to the New World when he was twenty-six was the only work he ever published.

Harriot left behind thousands of unpublished manuscript pages detailing his scientific and mathematical studies. What we know about Harriot's scientific work has come from studies of those manuscript pages by his contemporaries, his students and various historians and scientists down through the centuries. His work, which rivaled that of Kepler, Galileo, and Newton, remained largely unknown until recent times. Aside from the Harrioteers, as his modern admirers call themselves, few people have ever heard of Harriot, his role in the exploration of the New World, or his significant scientific and mathematical discoveries.

In these pages, we will explore the life of this fascinating man by looking at his education, his early affiliation with Sir Walter Ralegh, and his experimentation. We will also learn how his unorthodox scientific beliefs prevented him from publishing his work in England and nearly sent him to the gallows.

Early Life and Education

Thomas Harriot came from Oxfordshire—probably from St. Mary's parish in the city of Oxford, though there is no record of his birth or baptism. Most likely, his father was Thomas Harriot the blacksmith in the village of Clifton. He had land leases and a farm in Oxfordshire, was married to Joane Amay, and left a will in 1585. He named his brother John his executor; our Thomas Harriot had an uncle named John, so researchers have surmised that this blacksmith was Thomas' father.

In December 1577, Thomas Harriot and twelve other young men entered St. Mary Hall as new students at Oxford University. For a blacksmith's son growing up in Oxford, aspiring to attend the university was a very lofty goal. Harriot undoubtedly had a keen mind, and adults in his school and parish would have encouraged him to attend university. Tuition was set according to the family's ability to pay. The record shows that Harriot was a plebian (a commoner needing financial support), age 17, when he entered the university.

Higher-born young men more often attended Oriel College, adjacent to St. Mary Hall; today, both have merged into Oriel College of Oxford University. At the time he was there, Oxford University existed primarily to train clerics for the church or, for those such as Walter Ralegh, to give wealthy young men a veneer of education. Harriot progressed well beyond the normal studies at St. Mary Hall, excelling in mathematics and natural philosophy.

Mathematics and science—natural philosophy, as it was called then—generally did not appear in a young man's curriculum until completion of the three-year bachelor's degree. In fact, Protestant zealots frequently seized textbooks, particularly mathematics books that contained arcane symbols, and burned them on bonfires in Oxford's market place. The zealots believed those studies led to heresy or even witchcraft. Harriot would remember the superstition that such men held regarding the two subjects he found most interesting. These hostile attitudes may have contributed to his reluctance to publish his groundbreaking work in science and mathematics later in life.

While at Oxford, Harriot had the opportunity to hear lectures by Richard Hakluyt on the subject of geography, and lectures by Thomas Allen on mathematics and science. He made friends with both men and maintained ties with them throughout their lives. Allen's scientific laboratory, which Harriot saw when he visited his lodgings, prompted Harriot to assemble his own laboratory once he established himself in London in later years. His own theoretical studies and experimentation went well beyond what Allen achieved at Oxford. Richard Hakluyt spent his life encouraging English colonization of the New World, and he became a charter member of the London Company that sent colonists to Jamestown in 1606. From Hakluyt, Harriot developed his keen interest in applying mathematics to problems of navigation and mapmaking.

Harriot was one of only three of the original thirteen classmates to earn his degree. The degree, conferred in the spring of 1580, allowed Harriot to precede his name with the title "Master." Students and faculty at Oxford wore black clothing and caps, evoking the supposed costume of the Magi. For the rest of his life, Harriot habitually wore black clothing, consciously reinforcing his appearance as a seeker of wisdom. However, he didn't shun all fashion; he appeared in public wearing a rapier and a dagger—items no Elizabethan gentleman would be seen without. We don't know what Harriot looked like. Experts have discredited two portraits, widely published as Harriot, leaving his appearance solely to our imagination. Most likely, he wore a short-cropped beard, the fashion of the time. Given his dietary restraint, we can imagine that he was thin.

The headmasters at St. Mary Hall were fellows of Oriel College—Ralegh's college—and one of them may have recommended Master Thomas Harriot to Walter Ralegh. Ralegh had decided to establish a school for mariners at *Durham House* and was searching for a suitable instructor, one skilled in the application of mathematics to the problems of navigation. Just as likely, Richard Hakluyt connected Ralegh and Harriot. Hakluyt's compilation of the stories of English explorers and his conversations with Sir Francis Drake reinforced his belief that England needed to better prepare her mariners to compete with the Portuguese and Spanish. Once he had acquired *Durham House*, a suitable London location for training mariners, Walter Ralegh took up this challenge.

Sir Walter Ralegh's Man

After his graduation from Oxford in 1580, Harriot went to London, where he supported himself as a private tutor until 1583, when he began his long association with Sir Walter Ralegh as navigation instructor for Ralegh and his shipmasters. Ralegh paid Harriot an annual salary of £100 (four years salary for an artisan at that time) for this work and many other duties, including advice on shipbuilding, accounting, management of various business interests, and surveying Ralegh's extensive Irish properties.

Harriot's first priority had to be the science of navigation. In early 1584, Ralegh focused his attention on sending an expedition to North America to establish a colony there. Soon after joining Ralegh's household, Harriot read virtually every book available on navigation, particularly those published by the Portuguese and Spanish. Importantly, he also interviewed mariners on the London docks so that he could understand how they went about setting and maintaining their courses aboard ship. Thereby, he merged his theoretical knowledge with the practical knowledge of experienced shipmasters. That was his real genius—his ability to apply advanced mathematics to practical problems to achieve new approaches that would increase precision, lower risk, and yet prove useful to less-educated people.

At this time, Harriot also began his astronomical studies. He first observed the stars to produce more accurate star-position tables for use by navigators. Later, he would study the stars and planets as a true astronomer. For now, he developed tables of data for Polaris and for the sun that correlated their angle above the horizon with time and the observer's location on the Earth.

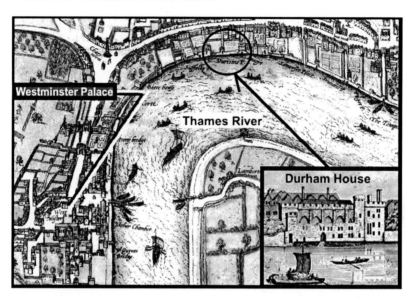

Durham House **where Harriot lived with Sir Walter Ralegh and taught navigation to Ralegh's mariners**

Then he turned his attention to the navigational instruments of the day. Aside from the compass, which gave the ship's heading, mariners used a cross-staff that allowed them to measure, with great difficulty, the elevation of the sun or a star above the horizon. Another device used for the same purpose was the astrolabe. Both devices had their drawbacks on a ship's pitching and rolling deck. Harriot made improvements in those instruments and instructed Ralegh and his shipmasters in the proper technique of taking sightings and determining the vessel's latitude from the astronomical tables he provided. Harriot compiled his training materials into a book he called "Arcticon." We know this privately-produced book existed for many years, but no copies survive today.

Following the Queen's granting of his American land patent in March 1584, Ralegh sent two ships to North America on his first expedition. A complete list of the members of the expedition doesn't exist. We know that Philip Amadas, Ralegh's cousin, led the expedition from his 200-ton ship, *Bark Ralegh*, and one of Ralegh's soldiers from his campaign in Ireland, Arthur Barlow, sailed the second, smaller ship, *Dorothy*, a fifty-ton pinnace. They departed Plymouth on April 27, 1584.

The state of the art of navigation at that time provided no accurate method of determining longitude. Accurate timepieces would be needed to solve that problem, and one wasn't invented until 1761 when John Harrison perfected the marine chronometer.

Sixteenth-Century Navigation

It is possible, and some think likely, that Thomas Harriot sailed on this expedition, but no records document that. This first, quick voyage established the route subsequent expeditions for Ralegh would take to North America: along the coast of Europe, down to the Canary Islands and then west until landfall in the Antilles. Once locating the Antilles, the ships followed that island chain north to Florida and then along the coast of America to what Ralegh came to call Virginia in honor of Elizabeth I, the Virgin Queen.

We know that this reconnoitering voyage included careful soundings of the waters along the east coast of North America and recording prominent geographical features to aid future mariners in locating Ralegh's colony. The two ships selected the Outer Banks of modern-day North Carolina as their proposed settlement site. Passing through an inlet south of Kill Devil Hills on 5 July, they found Roanoke Island. Having had a warm and cordial reception with the Indians living there, Amadas and Barlowe returned to England in the fall of 1584 and recommended to Ralegh that Roanoke Island was the preferred settlement site.

Whether or not Thomas Harriot made this first voyage to America, he would be a key member of the next expedition—Ralegh's first settlement of Englishmen in North America. The second expedition posed a much greater logistical challenge. Ralegh assembled 600 men with seven ships for this settlement attempt. Thomas Harriot would be responsible for the scientific study of the plants, animals, minerals, and native inhabitants of Virginia.

During the winter of 1584-1585, Harriot spent much of his time with the two Algonquian-speaking Indians, Manteo and Wanchese, who had returned with Arthur Barlowe on *Dorothy*. One reason to believe that Harriot sailed back to England with them on that first voyage is the level of fluency he had achieved in the Algonquian language by the beginning of 1585. It seems more likely that he had reached that level by having been with the Indians for the six months since landfall at the Outer Banks rather than just the short time since they had arrived in London. From his studies with the two Indians, Harriot compiled a dictionary of the Algonquian language, which he called "The Virginian Language." His dictionary manuscript existed until at least 1684, but is now lost.

Harriot's dictionary would be invaluable to linguists today if ever found. It may well have helped men such as Captain John Smith learn the Indian language before his voyage to Jamestown in 1607. Smith clearly had some mastery of the Algonquian language before his capture and confrontation with Powhatan in December 1607. Harriot would also have instructed George Percy, his patron's young brother, in the Indian language before Percy sailed with Smith to America.

Harriot's Algonquian Language Dictionary

Harriot had learned a great deal about the Indians' language and the geography of their homeland before leaving England on the second voyage. He sailed aboard *Tiger*, a 200-ton ship on loan from Queen Elizabeth. *Tiger* was the flagship, and the expedition commander, Sir Richard Grenville, along with the governor of the settlement, Colonel Ralph Lane, sailed aboard her. Manteo and Wanchese most likely sailed in company with Harriot. In addition, we know that John White, the expedition artist, sailed with them since his earliest pictures show scenes at Puerto Rico—a scheduled rendezvous for all seven ships—before any of the other ships had arrived there.

Detail from the Map of Virginia drawn by John White from Thomas Harriot's geographic data, showing the Outer Banks of North Carolina, the sounds, and the mainland beyond in remarkably accurate detail. North is to the right.

In Virginia, Harriot teamed with John White and the two Indians as he went about his tasks of identifying the animals, plants, and minerals of that area and talking to the Indians to learn as much as possible about their technology, culture, social structure, and religion. Harriot's *A Brief and True Report of the New Found Land of Virginia*, illustrated with engravings of John White's paintings, drawings, and maps, provides a surprisingly detailed account of what they found in the New

World with the help of Manteo and Wanchese. Harriot had a great respect for the intelligence, spirituality, and capability of the Native Americans. He devoted much of his time to exploring their religious beliefs and their social practices, and he admired their abstemiousness. He, too, ate and drank sparingly throughout his life.

Harriot's would be the only such scientific study of North America for many years. By the time of the Jamestown colony (twenty years later), the English were so focused on survival that studies of this nature would not take place for decades. Aside from Captain John Smith's map of the Chesapeake Bay and his short list of Algonquian words, no seventeenth-century explorers would come close to producing the careful, analytical observations made by Thomas Harriot in 1585-1586.

During his time as a member of this first English settlement in North America, Harriot traveled hundreds of miles into the mainland, following the sounds and rivers of the Outer Banks area. He spent the winter living with the Chesepioc Indians near modern-day Norfolk. His careful observations of geographic features accompanied by triangulation measurements allowed his associate, John White, to render highly accurate maps of the coastal and inland territory from the mouth of the Chesapeake Bay south to Cape Lookout (more than 200 miles of coast) and nearly one hundred miles inland.

In spite of Harriot's success, this first colony suffered due to the expedition leaders' inept dealings with the Indians. First, Sir Richard Grenville had the village of Aquascogoc burned in punishment for the alleged theft of a silver cup. Then Governor Ralph Lane led a number of raids on various Indian villages, which escalated from kidnapping an Indian weroance's son to assassinating Wingina, the principal leader of the Indians in the Roanoke Island area.

By June 1586, it was clear that the English were personae non gratae at the Outer Banks. Fortunately, Sir Francis Drake sailed in to check on their welfare and offered them assistance. They first planned to relocate to the Chesapeake Bay where Harriot had established good relations with the Indians, but when a hurricane blew into the Outer Banks, Harriot and the other first settlers wisely took the opportunity to sail away with Drake. They returned to England, leaving on June 18 and arriving at Portsmouth, England, July 28, 1586. This was Harriot's last trip to America. He could be justifiably proud of what he had achieved and would be able to point to his *Brief and True Report* with a sense of accomplishment. That material, reprinted in Latin and many European editions during his lifetime, remains in print and in demand today.

Sir Walter Ralegh sent a second expedition to America in 1587. By this time, Harriot and others had advised a fresh start among the Chesepioc Indians where they had found safer harbors for large ships and anticipated friendlier relations with the Native Americans. Harriot's associate, John White, led this expedition, but because of the treachery of his piratical ship's master, 115 men, women, and children found themselves abandoned at Roanoke Island instead of the intended Chesapeake Bay location. They became the "Lost Colonists" when, in 1588, the Spanish Armada's attack on England interrupted the flow of supplies to Ralegh's new colony.

Harriot lived at Molanna Abbey in Ireland from 1586 to 1589, surveying Ralegh's 40,000-acre estate in Munster. Ralegh granted him the abbey for his use while in Ireland. Harriot had no apparent role in Ralegh's attempts at colonization of North America after his return with Drake's fleet; however, he assisted Ralegh with the logistics of his various colonization efforts during the years 1587 to 1616. Harriot returned to London after his survey work in Ireland was complete and lived there the rest of his life, first at *Durham House* and later at *Syon House*, the riverfront home of Henry Percy, the Ninth Earl of Northumberland.

During the last decade of the sixteenth century, Harriot performed a number of studies for Ralegh. In addition to developing the star tables for navigators, he determined how to establish local magnetic variation from observations of the angular altitude of the sun. He also developed spherical geometry to accurately locate points on the globe and portray the size of geographical areas independent of their latitude— solving the so-called "Mercator Problem." Harriot's mastery of spherical geometry was decades ahead of other mathematicians.

Ralegh put Harriot to work on several other practical problems. For example, Harriot calculated how many cannon balls could be stacked in a specific deck area. Then he worked on ways to improve the accuracy of gunners aboard English ships. Orthodox belief, based on the theories of Aristotle supported by the church, held that solid objects in space fall toward the center of the Earth at a speed proportional to their weight. Aristotle taught that objects traveled in straight lines or circles, thus cannon balls would move in a straight line under the force of the powder explosion, and once that had abated, would fall to earth in a circular motion. Existing ballistic tables, based on this mistaken belief, therefore had built-in aiming errors. Harriot studied the problem, interviewed experienced gunners, and correctly concluded that cannon balls travel in a parabolic course. He also correctly observed that the time of ascent of a cannon ball fired above the horizontal equals the time of descent. He provided improved tables for the English gunners' use.

Ralegh also set Harriot to examine the current state of ship design. The premier shipbuilder in England at this time was Matthew Baker, Queen Elizabeth's first designated "Master Shipwright." Baker used a number of rules of thumb to determine breadth, length, draft, mast height, and other characteristic dimensions of the ships he built. Harriot made detailed measurements of a variety of ships known for their speed and sailing ability. He also interviewed shipmasters to get their viewpoint on ship handling characteristics. From his studies, he developed theoretical mathematical formulas that aided shipbuilders like Baker in producing superior hull designs.

In 1593, Henry Percy, the Ninth Earl of Northumberland, met Thomas Harriot through his friendship with Sir Walter Ralegh. The earl, four years younger than Harriot, had a strong interest in all intellectual pursuits. Harriot's wideranging studies fascinated him. Northumberland was one of the wealthiest men in England and high in the order of succession for the crown of England. The earl offered Harriot a stipend of £80 per year and a house on his *Syon* estate in which to live and set up a scientific laboratory. Later the earl increased Harriot's "pension" to £100 per year. Because of his pursuit of science, albeit as an informed amateur, some called Henry Percy the "Wizard Earl." Percy surrounded himself with men who shared his intellectual interests. Harriot was preeminent among those associates, and the Wizard Earl gladly provided Harriot sufficient money to pursue his scientific and mathematical studies.

Harriot continued to work for Ralegh and eventually took charge of some responsibilities for the earl, although their relationship remained more one of friends than employer and employee. Harriot maintained a presence in the household of both of his patrons, traveling by boat the three hours between their Thames River homes: *Durham House* and *Syon House.*

Scientific Discoveries

Soon after joining Walter Ralegh at *Durham House,* Harriot erected an astronomical platform on the roof so that he could observe the motion of the stars, the moon, the sun, and the planets. He made his earliest observations with a twelve-foot long cross-staff, recording the angular position of the celestial objects at various times of day. He kept meticulous notes of his observations in journals. Harriot was the first Englishman to design and build a telescope, which he used to make the first English astronomical studies. Beginning in the summer of 1609, he used a variety of telescopes of his own design to examine the surface of the moon, the appearance of the planets, and the surface of the sun. From his studies, he discovered that the sun had dark spots—sunspots—that moved over its surface. He identified sunspots for the first time in the western world.

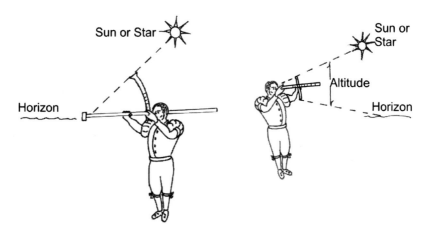

Harriot invented the back-staff, an improvement over the cross staff that required the user to look toward the sun. Back-staff is on the left.

He also charted the craters and other features he saw on the moon with the aid of his telescope. In 1610, he observed the motion of the moons of Jupiter. His observations in some cases preceded those of Galileo and in other cases, followed Galileo's by only a few months. Because Galileo quickly published his results, he, not Harriot, is known as the first great pioneer in the new science of astronomy.

Galileo learned of the Dutch invention of the telescope in June of 1609 and had his first telescope the first week in July; Harriot was making observations of the moon with his own telescope on July 26, 1609. Thus, the two astronomers began their work almost simultaneously and independently. Harriot's friends chided him on his failure to publish his important discoveries.

His friend and student Sir William Lower wrote to him in 1610:

Doe you not here startle to see every day some of your inventions taken from you; for I remember long since you told me as much, that the motions of the planets were not perfect circles. So you taught me the curious way to observe weight in Water and within a while after Ghetaldi come out with it, in print, a little before Vieta prevented you of the Gharland for the great Invention of Algebra.

Harriot learned from his own observations that the planets' orbits are elliptical rather than circular. Johannes Kepler would ultimately get credit for that discovery. Harriot also made extensive experimental measurements of the specific gravity of many substances by immersing samples in water and observing the weight and volume of water displaced. That data has been found tabulated in his journals, ready for publication, yet Harriot hesitated, and so Marino Ghetaldi received the credit in 1603. François Viete published his treatise on algebra in 1591, years after Harriot had developed his advanced algebra, which was mathematically more complete and complex than Viete's algebra.

One facet of Harriot's research that shows his advanced mathematical ability and his careful development of scientific theory is his study of the refraction of light. In the 1590s, he applied himself to the study of how light rays bend as they pass through a translucent material such as glass. By 1597, he had built an apparatus in his laboratory that allowed him to measure the angles of incidence and refraction, calculating the angle that light rays bend to a high degree of accuracy. He produced tables of data for various materials and then discovered the mathematical relationship between the angles. He expressed that relationship using trigonometry as: the sine of the angle of incidence equals a constant times the sine of the angle of refraction. The constant is the refractive index of the material the light has passed through. Unfortunately, Harriot didn't publish his groundbreaking work on optics. In 1621, Willebrord Snell received credit for discovering that law of optics. Today it is known as Snell's Law—not Harriot's Law.

Harriot also observed how different colors of light are refracted at different angles—most evident when light passes through a prism. He exchanged letters with Johannes Kepler on this subject but kept his theory to himself. He believed, rightly, that light interacts with the atomic structure of the prism. Kepler clearly admired Harriot's ability as a mathematician and a physicist (a term that did not exist at that time). He questioned Harriot on the origin of colors. Harriot pleaded illness to avoid answering, and in one letter told Kepler, "our situation is such that I still may not philosophize freely; we are still stuck in the mud." He was clearly afraid to publish his scientific and mathematical work: but why? We will learn how his scientific beliefs and his controversial associates caused his fear.

His research into the refractive index and density of various materials led him to speculate that atomic structure determined the various physical properties of all substances. Harriot believed in atomism—the idea that all matter is composed of invisible particles that join in unique ways, determining the physical properties of every substance. The atomistic theory dated back to Leucippus and Democritus in ancient Greece.

Harriot believed that atoms were indestructible and eternal. He argued that nothing could be created from nothing—a position considered heretical by church officials who taught that God created the universe out of the void. Harriot's notes reveal that he attributed all the effects of nature to the local motion of atoms or bodies made of atoms. This theory underlay his experiments in alchemy in 1599 and 1600, his measurements of specific gravity of various substances, and his optical experiments. However, atomism equated to atheism in the minds of church leaders at that time. Bishop Lancelot Andrews preached, "...moral matters may not looke for Mathematical proofes." The established

17

Church of England clearly denounced the new scientific rationalism that Harriot practiced.

The Church of England and the Roman Catholic Church considered atomism a heretical belief. Giordano Bruno, who had lived in London for a time and who had been in the circle of Ralegh, Henry Percy, Harriot and others, shared Harriot's beliefs about the universe and atomism. In 1600, after seven years in prison, Bruno paid for his scientific beliefs with his life when church authorities in Rome tied him naked to a stake in the square and burned him to death.

Syon House, Home of the Ninth Earl of Northumberland, About twelve miles upstream from Ralegh's Durham House

Galileo also feared the charge of heresy. In 1597, he wrote to Kepler, "Many years ago I was converted to the Theory of Copernicus …. But I have not yet dared to publish them [his reasons for that belief]. I am thoroughly frightened by the plight of our master Copernicus …. I would surely have the courage to make my thinking public if there were more people like you." Galileo eventually published his controversial views in 1632, and the Church of Rome summarily imprisoned him. He remained under house arrest for the rest of his life, even though he recanted his belief in the sun-centered universe—a belief Harriot also held. It is easy to see how Harriot would have been reluctant to publish his own theories and research data. His fears of the English authorities were well founded.

Additional pioneering work of Harriot included the development of a binary number theory—the basis of digital computing that pervades modern technology. He also developed some of the mathematical symbols used in modern notation, such as the radical sign signifying roots ($\sqrt{}$), and the symbols used for greater than and less than ($>$ $<$) in mathematical expressions. At the end of the sixteenth century, Harriot enjoyed some fame in Europe as an accomplished mathematician. His failure to publish his work prevented him from getting the lasting credit he deserved; nonetheless, he avoided the fate of Bruno and Galileo.

Nicolaus Copernicus rejected the idea that the earth was at the center of the universe and proposed the sun as the center of the universe, around which the earth and the other planets rotated. He correctly postulated that earth has a daily rotation, a yearly rotation around the sun, and the earth's axis rotates over a much longer period. He also said that the distance from the earth to the sun was small in comparison to the distance to the stars.

These ideas starkly contradicted the traditional Ptolemaic system accepted by the church that viewed the earth as an immobile center around which heavenly spheres carried the stars, the sun, the moon and the planets.

Copernicus' work on astronomy, *De revolutionibus orbium coelestium*, was published at the end of his seventy-year life; he received his copy the day he died, May 24, 1543. The Catholic Church judged his book heretical and banned it. The Church of England viewed it the same way.

Rejection of the Geocentric Universe

Accusations of Heresy and Atheism

Thomas Harriot had the good fortune to meet many exciting people through his association with Sir Walter Ralegh. Through Ralegh, he had met and eventually joined the household of Henry Percy. Ralegh and Percy often dined together, and gambled together, and Harriot frequently joined them. He also met Giordano Bruno, playwright Christopher Marlowe, Dr. John Dee (royal astrologer, alchemist, mathematician and, some believed, magician) and the noted poet, Edmund Spenser. Harriot also came to know and correspond with one of the most influential men in England, Robert Cecil, Lord Salisbury. Cecil, Secretary of State and principal advisor to the crown, appeared to be a friend of Ralegh, Percy, and Harriot, but later he made his true feelings apparent, with disastrous consequences for all three.

Because of Harriot's close association with Ralegh and Percy, his reputation was linked to theirs. To avoid public censure and the political intrigues of his courtly patrons, Harriot maintained his privacy at *Durham House* and *Syon*, serving Ralegh and Percy faithfully but avoiding as much as possible a public position. He preferred to spend his time in scholarly pursuits when not dealing with Ralegh's business affairs in England and Ireland or tutoring various students at the Percy home.

In 1592, Ralegh, who had enjoyed the principal place among Queen Elizabeth's courtiers, fell from her grace. She discovered that he had secretly married one of her ladies-in-waiting, Elizabeth Throckmorton, and Bess, as she was known, had given birth to a son. The queen was furious. On August 7, without a trial, the queen threw Ralegh and his wife into the Tower of London. The Raleghs were soon released, but Sir Walter would never enjoy the degree of familiarity and support he had formerly had with Queen Elizabeth. Other courtiers, jealous of Ralegh's influence over the queen, sensed that they could now attack and further damage his reputation.

An early attack came from an unusual direction. Father Robert Parsons, a Jesuit priest, had denounced Queen

Elizabeth as a heretic. Parsons' denouncement of the queen, published in Augsburg in 1592, also attacked Ralegh and Harriot. He referred to Ralegh as follows:

> *Of Sir Walter Rawley's Schoole of Atheisme by the waye, and of the Conjurer that is Master thereof, and of the diligence used to get young gentlemen to the schoole, wherein both Moyses and our savior, the olde and the new Testaments are jested at, and the schollers taught amonge other things, to spell God backwarde ....*

The master to whom Parsons referred could be none other than Thomas Harriot. Parsons was not the first to question Ralegh's religious beliefs. Ralegh had associated himself with many free thinkers such as Bruno and Marlowe. Harriot certainly was present and presumably contributed to the conversations on philosophy, religion, and politics that took place at Ralegh's homes and later at Henry Percy's household. At times, churchmen would take part in these dinnertime conversations, and they would find themselves expected to defend church doctrine in light of the new scientific discoveries. While Ralegh enjoyed the queen's favor, he could get away with these dangerous conversations. However, when she pushed him away from her inner circle, he found himself vulnerable and his close associate, Harriot, became guilty by association.

On May 18, 1593, the Privy Council ordered Christopher Marlowe arrested on a charge of atheism. The evidence, hearsay though it was, linked Marlowe to Ralegh and Harriot. Preliminary evidence gathered from interviews before the interrogation of Marlowe consisted of nineteen points painting Marlowe as a blasphemer, calling into question the morality of Jesus Christ, his mother, and Christ's disciples. The material also included the following comments about Ralegh and Harriot:

> *That the Indians and many Authors of antiquity have assuredly written of about 16 thousand yeares agone where Adam is proved to have lived within 6 thousand years.* [Harriot would have been the source of Indian beliefs. The church held that God created Adam, the first man, 6,000 years in the

past. Harriot probably didn't believe that part of church doctrine.]

He [Marlowe] affirmeth that Moyses was but a Jugler, & that one Heriots being Sir W. Raleighs man can do more than he.

That all they that love not Tobacco & Boies were fooles. [Harriot and Ralegh were viewed as bringing tobacco into court circles, and Marlowe was thought to be a homosexual].

Before Marlowe could be interrogated, however, he was murdered, stabbed above the right eye with a dagger by Ingram Frizer on May 30, 1593. Some have speculated that Sir Walter Ralegh had something to do with Marlowe's death. Whether or not Ralegh played a role in that very controversial crime, the charges of atheism went away for a while, but would resurface repeatedly.

The year before, in 1592, another publication had attacked Harriot. *Pierce Penilesse his supplication to the devill* stated, "I hear say there be Mathematicians [here] that will prove men [existed] before Adam, and they are harbored in high places, who will maintain it to the death, that there are no devils…" The mathematician referred to in this piece by Thomas Nashe was Thomas Harriot.

In March of 1594, Ralegh and his family were living at *Sherborne Abbey,* his estate in Dorset. Harriot was living in London at *Syon House* at this time, a guest of Henry Percy. An official inquiry was conducted at Cerne Abbas from 21 to 28 March regarding "impious opinions concerning God and Providence" attributed to Walter Ralegh and "his man" Thomas Harriot. No charges resulted from this inquiry that consisted of more hearsay evidence offered by church officials and local citizens.

Sir Walter Ralegh sailed to Guiana in 1595, leaving Harriot to manage his business affairs while he was away. Ralegh had invested £80,000 of his own funds in his quest to find El Dorado in the South American highlands. That gives some measure of the magnitude of the financial affairs Harriot oversaw for Ralegh on a number of occasions. It also indicates the level of trust Ralegh placed in Harriot. Harriot never let his friend Ralegh down.

Harriot conducted Ralegh's affairs competently and didn't shrink from going to the highest official in Queen Elizabeth's court when necessary. While Ralegh was absent, this time leading a raid against the Spanish at Cadiz, Harriot wrote to Robert Cecil, Lord Salisbury, emphasizing the good that had come from Ralegh's expedition to Guiana and expressing concern that some of Ralegh's loose-tongued shipmasters might disclose strategically important geographical data to the Spanish. Cecil acted on Harriot's advice and had the maps in the shipmasters' possession confiscated and the men warned not to divulge the data. While Harriot and Ralegh may have taken this as a sign of Cecil's loyalty to them, they were mistaken. Cecil looked to his own interest first and then to that of the crown. For the time being, his true feelings about Ralegh remained hidden.

Eight years later, Ralegh's star fell again, this time due to the death of his queen. In the last few years of Elizabeth's reign, courtiers began to look for her successor. Robert Cecil conducted secret negotiations with King James VI of Scotland, his choice to succeed Elizabeth. So did Henry Percy. At this time, Cecil attacked Northumberland by writing to James VI that Percy could not be trusted, that Percy was James' enemy; he portrayed Sir Walter Ralegh in a similar way.

However, Northumberland's own secret correspondence with King James proved effective, at least for a time. When Elizabeth died on March 24, 1603, James VI of Scotland became James I of England. During the king's triumphal procession into London, Henry Percy rode in honor at the right side of the new king. Percy also received a position on King James' Privy Council. But Cecil, the new king's principal adviser, would continue to work in secret to eliminate Ralegh and Percy from court.

Cecil attacked Ralegh first. By May, Ralegh had orders to vacate *Durham House,* and soon lost his other financially lucrative honors. By July, Ralegh found himself back in the Tower of London, this time charged with treason. The charges made no sense, but a special court convened at Winchester went through the motions, allowing Ralegh to attempt to defend himself. Harriot assisted Ralegh by researching the law on treason. He found a passage that seemed to ensure that someone couldn't be convicted of treason on the basis of only one witness. The court had produced only one witness, and he had provided the testimony only after torture. Nonetheless, the court found Ralegh guilty. Lord Chief Justice Popham, prior to sentencing Ralegh, provided the following advice

> *Yow know what men say of Harriot. Yow should doe well before yow goe out of this world to give satisfaction herein, and not to die with those imputations in yow. Let not any devil persuade yow to think there is no eternitie in hell fire.*

Once again, Harriot's name was mentioned as one who had led Ralegh to accept atheism as his creed. Popham then sentenced Ralegh to be hanged, drawn, and quartered. However, King James stayed the execution for the time being.

Ralegh would live most of the rest of his life as a prisoner in the Tower, albeit in relative luxury, under a delayed death sentence. Harriot would call on Ralegh frequently at the Tower, assisting Ralegh with his writing and his studies of science, and seeing to the business affairs that Ralegh needed help with. Although stripped of his honors, Ralegh still had lucrative, income-producing properties, and he continued to pay Harriot an annual pension of £100.

Harriot's religious belief, or supposed non-belief, caused him great difficulty throughout his life. However, Harriot appears from his writing and other sources to have followed Church of England doctrine in general. He believed in God, the Trinity, and adhered to church practices during his life. As a young man, Harriot read from the Bible to Indians in North America and taught them about Christianity. It seems clear that at age twenty-six, when he was among the Indians in America, Harriot was an adherent to the Church of England.

A letter from his good friend, Sir William Lower, sheds some light on Harriot's religious beliefs. Following the death of Lower's son, he wrote to Harriot, "I have learnt [from] you to settle and submit my desires to the will of god...." Late in life, Harriot wrote to a physician, "I believe in one almighty God; I believe in the art of medicine as ordained by him; I believe in the physician as his minister." Finally, in the preamble to his last will and testament, he clearly demonstrated his belief in God and the principle of the Trinity.

Today, we would call Harriot a skeptic, not an atheist. For him, truth came from scientific experimentation and rational analysis—practices feared and discouraged by the established church during Harriot's lifetime. Nevertheless, his scientific pursuits and his association with Walter Ralegh and Henry Percy, two men with high visibility and important political enemies, would continue to sully Harriot's reputation.

Robert Cecil, the most powerful of political enemies, now turned his attention to the Earl of Northumberland, Henry Percy. On November 5, 1605, Cecil got the chance he needed to dispose of Northumberland. Cecil's agents caught the men plotting to blow up Parliament, assassinate King James, and restore a Roman Catholic monarch to the English throne in what we now call the Gunpowder Plot. Northumberland's cousin, Thomas Percy, a central figure in the conspiracy and a suspected Papist, had rented the house near Parliament from which the plotters had planned to tunnel under the building where Parliament met. When the tunnel proved infeasible, Thomas Percy rented a basement in the Parliament building directly under where King James would ceremonially open the next session of Parliament.

Although Henry Percy appeared to have no knowledge of the Gunpowder Plot, his cousin Thomas had dined with him on 4 November, and Thomas Harriot attended that dinner.

In addition, Percy's uncle had led a Catholic uprising in the north, and Queen Elizabeth had him executed for rebellion. Furthermore, Henry Percy had advised King James to be lenient on English Catholics in order to ensure their support of his monarchy. Therefore, Henry Percy appeared to King James, with Cecil's whispered encouragement, to be a secret Papist out to bring down the king.

Cecil, having received advance notice of the plot, had his men waiting, and late on 4 November, they caught Guy Fawkes, the explosive expert, with fuses to ignite the thirty-three barrels of gunpowder under Parliament. Fawkes, only hours before, had met with Thomas Percy at *Syon House*. Under interrogation, the names of the other conspirators soon came forth. Thomas Percy escaped and avoided capture for a few days, but Cecil's men found and killed him before anyone could interrogate him.

Henry Percy was under house arrest. On 27 November, guards moved the Earl of Northumberland to the Tower of London. He would remain there for sixteen years. Two days before Percy's transfer to the Tower, they arrested Thomas Harriot and locked him in the Gatehouse Prison at Westminster. On 12 December, Harriot wrote an appeal to Robert Cecil, pleading his innocence with regard to the Gunpowder Plot. Cecil never replied. In desperation, Harriot wrote to the Privy Council the following letter on 16 December.

Right honorable my very good Lordes:

The present misery I feele being truly innocent in hart and thought presseth me to be an humble suter to your lordships for favorable respect. All that know me can witness that I was always of honest conversation and life. I was never any busy meddler in matters of state. I was never ambitious for preferments. But contented with a private life for the love of learning that I might study freely. Wherein my labours & endevours, if I may speak it without praesumption, have ben painfull & great. And I hoped & do yet hope by the grace of God & your Lordships favour that the effectes shall so shew themselves shortly, to the good liking &

allowance of the state and common weale. But now this misery of close imprisonment happening unto me at the time of my sickness, which was more then three weeks old before; being great windenes in my stomack & fumings into my head rising from my spleen, besides other infirmityes, as my Doctor knoweth & some effectes my keeper can witness. This I say without your honours favour wil be my utter undoing, not only in respect of great charges, greater then I am able to endure; but also of being in place where I am not likely to recover health. Therefore the innocency of my hart feeling this misery of close imprisonment with sicknes & many wantes, besides the desire of proceeding in my studies, maketh me an humble suter to your honours for liberty in what measure your wisedomes shall think fit. So shall I with faythfull acknowledgement spend the rest of my time so, that your honours shall not think any lawfull favour ill bestowed. And I shall as my bounden duty is continue my dayly prayers to almighty god for the preservation of his Majesty and Royall progeny, and for the encrease of all honor and happiness to your honors. Your honors humble petitioner:

A poore prisoner in the gatehouse

Tho: Harriots

Harriot had been accused of casting a horoscope of King James so that the Earl of Northumberland would know how long the king would reign and when he would die. This alleged act seemed to trouble the King more than any implications that Northumberland or Harriot had actually known about the plot to kill him. It was as if the act of casting the horoscope might have had some effect on the health of the sovereign—typical of the superstitious thinking of James and his court.

His letter apparently persuaded the Privy Council. He was back in residence in his house at *Syon* by the spring of 1606. Just as easily, his fate could have been a death sentence. The next year, he calculated the orbit of a newly observed comet—later called Halley's Comet—based on his own measurements taken with a cross-staff. Over the next few years, he would have his most productive period as an astronomer.

His Final Years

From 1606 until his death, Thomas Harriot continued to receive his pensions from Ralegh and Percy—£100 from each until Ralegh's death in 1618. Harriot visited his friends Ralegh and Percy at their lavish prison quarters at the Tower of London. Both men continued their interest in science, and Harriot kept them supplied with the materials and equipment they needed. During this period, Harriot built telescopes, which he called "perspective trunks," and made discoveries that should have given him at least an equal place alongside Galileo in the new science of astronomy.

Beginning in 1605, Harriot employed a laboratory assistant. Christopher Tooke assisted him by grinding lenses for the telescopes Harriot built, and Tooke assembled other equipment such as the forerunner of the spectroscope that Harriot designed to study the dispersion of light into color bands. Harriot has been called "the first experimental physicist" of the modern age.

From his observation of Jupiter's moons, Harriot knew that the earth didn't sit at the center of the universe. Those moons orbiting another planet made it clear to Harriot that the church-sanctioned idea, originating with Aristotle, of an unblemished sun and planets orbiting the earth in perfect circular paths, was nonsense. He must have found it maddeningly frustrating not to publish his own theories of the universe, grounded in his careful observations. Apparently, his brief incarceration had ended any thoughts he might have had to publish during his lifetime. Harriot satisfied himself to some extent by sharing his data and his scientific viewpoints with his closest students and his two wealthy patrons.

During the last nine years of his life, a number of Harriot's close friends died. Henry Stuart, Prince of Wales, died at age 18 in 1612. The prince had been a close associate of Sir Walter Ralegh, with whom he frequently met at the Tower of London. Cape Henry at the mouth of the

Chesapeake Bay bears this young prince's name. His death affected Ralegh more than Harriot, perhaps, but Harriot mourned the loss of this very bright young man who had decried his father's treatment of Ralegh. John Harrington, an aristocratic young student of Harriot at *Syon House,* died in 1614. Harriot had great hopes for this young man as well, and his loss began an inexorable emotional decline as more men important in Harriot's life died.

William Lower, a lifelong friend with whom he shared his passion for mathematics and astronomy, died in 1615. Lower's correspondence with Harriot has yielded important information on Harriot's work and helps date some of his discoveries.

Perhaps the biggest blow to Harriot came with the beheading of his long-time friend and patron, Sir Walter Ralegh. Briefly, Ralegh had convinced King James in 1616 that he could lead an expedition back to Guiana to find the gold of El Dorado. James desperately needed money by that time and agreed to release Ralegh to make the voyage. However, he stacked the deck against Ralegh by demanding that he sail into that Spanish held region but do nothing to offend the Spanish in his acquisition of the gold.

This difficult mission became mission impossible when James informed the Spanish ambassador of Ralegh's sailing plans and the strength of his fleet. When the fleet reached Guiana, Ralegh was too ill to participate. He sent his oldest son ashore with an armed force to capture the town where they believed a gold mine existed. His son, Wat, died in the first charge, and a number of the Spanish died as well. When news of the disastrous battle reached Ralegh, he realized that he had failed and broken his agreement with the king. Ralegh sailed back to England broken in spirit to tell his wife Bess of their son's death and to await his own death sentence. James ordered the execution of the old but still valid sentence passed on Ralegh for treason in 1603, but the king showed some mercy by allowing him to be beheaded rather than hanged, drawn and quartered.

Thomas Harriot visited Sir Walter Ralegh and Bess at the Tower the night before Ralegh's execution, offering what solace he could. The next day, October 29, 1618, he stood sadly among the onlookers in Whitehall as Ralegh made his final address to the assembled crowd and then bravely bent his head to the executioner's axe. Harriot left a summary of Ralegh's final words among his journals.

Harriot soon abandoned his scientific experiments. Sensing his own end was not far off, he spent his time putting his papers in order. More than 9,000 folio pages of Harriot's notes remain in the British Museum and at *Petworth House*, one of Northumberland's country estates. Very few of his journals bear dates after 1615. He clearly hoped that someone would eventually publish his papers. His hope would be partly fulfilled ten years after his death with the publication of *Artis Analyticae Praxis ad Aequationes Algebraicas*, a book on algebra assembled from a small portion of Harriot's mathematical journals. Many mathematical innovations remained lost in his journals awaiting discovery in recent times by modern investigators.

Thomas Harriot had a cancerous lesion on his left nostril. It started as a small spot perhaps as early as 1612, but by 1618 the lesion had grown large and had spread from his nose to his upper lip, affecting his breathing and speech. He consulted a number of physicians, starting with Sir Walter Ralegh's doctor. In 1615, Harriot consulted with the most important physician in England, Theodore de Mayerne, King James' personal doctor. De Mayerne recommended surgical removal of the lesion, which he attributed to Harriot's twenty years of smoking tobacco. For some reason Harriot didn't take that course. By 1620, he felt considerable discomfort and consulted with Dr. Alexander Read, who concluded that the cancer had advanced too far. Dr. Read could only offer some help for the pain.

Death came to Thomas Harriot on July 2, 1621 as he lay at the house of Thomas Buckner on Threadneedle Street near the Royal Exchange. Thirty-six years earlier, Buckner had sailed with Harriot to Virginia. Harriot had dictated his will on June 29, leaving his largest monetary bequest to his laboratory assistant Christopher Tooke, whom he called Kit. His household at *Syon* included Tooke, a butler, a housekeeper and an assistant housekeeper. All received bequests from Harriot.

Harriot had amassed a considerable estate over the years from the pensions he received from Ralegh and Percy and from their grants of property that produced additional income for him. His gambling with them perhaps added to his wealth. He lived simply, dressed plainly, and spent little on food or drink. His largest expenses were payments to his household staff and his purchases of materials for his scientific experiments.

In his will he directed that his papers be maintained, compiled, and whatever was deemed worthy be published. Aside from the brief book of his algebra, the administrators of his estate failed to publish his significant achievements in science or mathematics. The papers reverted to the estate of the Earl of Northumberland according to the terms of Harriot's will. For a century and a half, they lay abandoned. In 1660, the newly established Royal Society sought to locate and study Harriot's papers. His fame as a mathematician at that time was known and society members anticipated that Harriot had done other pioneering work, but they didn't obtain his papers.

In 1784, an Austrian named Baron von Zach visited *Petworth*. Von Zach discovered the Harriot papers there and offered to compile them for publication at Oxford University. At that time, some of Harriot's discoveries in astronomy and mathematics became known, but Oxford did not publish the Harriot papers. The manuscripts languished, divided, re-arranged, and left in a state of confusion. Eventually, they reverted to the Northumberland estate; the British Museum acquired some of the papers, but the rest remained at *Petworth*.

In the twentieth century, the papers finally received careful analysis by experts in mathematics, science, and history, and thus the true contributions of Thomas Harriot finally began to emerge. His reputation grows as those studies continue. Oxford University, Durham University, and the University of Delaware have held Thomas Harriot seminars every few years since the 1970s. Papers presented at these seminars have revealed Thomas Harriot's pioneering work and have placed that work in the larger context of science, mathematics, and society in the decades of his life. In America, Harriot's legacy is honored near where he conducted his groundbreaking explorations of the New World: at the Thomas Harriot College of Arts and Sciences, a division of East Carolina University, in Greenville, North Carolina.

Stay, traveler, lightly tread;
Near this spot lies that was mortal
Of that most celebrated man
THOMAS HARRIOT
He was that most learned Harriot
Of Syon on the River Thames;
By birth and education
An Oxonian
Who cultivated all the sciences
And excelled in all
In Mathematics, Natural Philosophy, Theology,
A most studious searcher after truth,
A most devout worshipper of the Triune God,
At the age of sixty, or thereabouts,
He bade farewell to mortality, not to life.
The Year of our Lord, 1621, July 2.

The Earl of Northumberland's Memorial to Thomas Harriot

On July 3, 1621, Thomas Buckner saw to the burial of his friend Thomas Harriot. Harriot's grave at St. Christopher-le-Stocks Church had a memorial plaque erected by his friend and patron, Henry Percy. The church burned in the Great Fire of London in 1666, destroying the plaque, but we have a published version of the text of the earl's memorial to Harriot. The church no longer exists, and the Bank of England expanded into the site. However, a reproduction of Percy's memorial plaque now hangs in the foyer of the bank.

One of the world's finest mathematicians, perhaps the first modern English scientist, the first scientific explorer of English North America, lies in an unmarked grave somewhere nearby.

Aleck Loker

Calvert's Bold Adventure
Human Rights and
Democracy in America

Chapter 2
Calvert's Bold Adventure
Human Rights and Democracy in America

In the early 17th century, an English colony in America became the testing ground for radical political experiments in human rights. A number of political "firsts" are identified with the colony of Maryland: first practice of religious toleration; first admission of an African American to an English-speaking legislature; first petition for the right to vote by a woman in America. The Maryland colony, founded by Lord Baltimore, was distinguished by many other activities that set precedents: for example, the first Baroque town plan, preceding the layout of Annapolis by sixty years. However, this booklet deals with the ground-breaking political activities that took place in St. Mary's City, the first capital of Maryland, founded in 1634.

England in the 16th and 17th Centuries

To understand the importance of the events at St. Mary's City, first we need to understand what life was like in England in the late 16th and early 17th centuries. England was a monarchy ruled by a succession of strong Tudor and Stuart kings and queens. War with Spain had ended, but tensions between those powers and with France dominated international politics. Exploration of the new world of the Americas created a vast opportunity for all three nations and contributed to the tensions among them.

Explorers and mapmakers had not determined the geographic extent of the Americas. Maps at the beginning of the 17th century depicted the east coast of North America roughly, but conjecturally showed the western coast relatively close to the east coast with the vast, unknown Western Sea uncharted. Explorers still hoped for an inland passage to the

Western Sea (the Pacific), which they hoped would provide a practical trade route to the Orient.

The Tudor monarchs had oppressive statutes enacted by Parliament, making Anglicanism the state religion and restricting the practice of other Protestant or Roman Catholic faiths. In fact, Roman Catholic priests could be executed for the treasonous act of setting foot on English soil. Catholics in England in 1633 numbered 60,000 out of a population of about 4,000,000. Even under the relatively benevolent reigns of James I and Charles I, the approximately 600 priest who ministered to English Catholics did so at some peril.

Those two monarchs, both of whom were married to Roman Catholics, permitted the practice of Catholicism as long as it was done in private. As far back as the time of Henry VIII, the Catholic Church in England land placed land they controlled in complicated trust arrangements to circumvent statutes prohibiting land ownership. Roman Catholic gentry commonly had chapels adjacent to or as part of their manor houses, and priests served them and their associates in those private "chapel-house" settings.

Each English person had a place in the hierarchy of society in the 17th century—the higher up the social scale, the more privilege and responsibility. This carried over into their legislative process.

Parliament consisted, as it does now, of two houses: the House of Lords, and the House of Commons. Members of the upper house were generally hereditary peers, Anglican bishops, and persons recently elevated to the aristocracy. From our perspective today, we would think that the members of the House of Commons were elected by the general population to represent various subdivisions of the country.

However, that is far from the truth. The House of Commons consisted of approximately 460 members of the gentry—those one rung lower on the social ladder than the peers—due to their relative wealth and influence, representing a very small percentage of the population. Very few of the members of the House of Commons owed their seat to an electoral process. An individual's participation in the House of Commons was due to his residence in a particular locale and his well-established influence or power in that area.

Elections to choose a Parliamentary representative were very rare. Parliament in the early part of the century was therefore more a council for the monarch than the democratic institution we know it to be today.

George Calvert, Father of Maryland

George Calvert, the first Lord Baltimore, deserves our great admiration for his achievements and the legacy he left us. He rose from relatively modest beginnings in Yorkshire as the eldest son of Leonard Calvert, a yeoman farmer. George Calvert received his degree from Trinity College, Oxford in 1597 and then entered Lincoln's Inn in August 1598. In London, He made the acquaintance of Sir Robert Cecil, a member of Queen Elizabeth's Privy Council.

George Calvert, 1ˢᵗ Lord Baltimore, Details from Gerard Soest portrait

By 1603, George was employed as Sir Robert's secretary. In the succeeding years, George Calvert used his access and growing skills in the royal court to become a highly regarded and influential member of the royal inner circle. He subsequently served James I as one of his principal secretaries of state and as a member of the Privy Council.

During his rise to prominence, Calvert invested in numerous colonial enterprises, and consequently we may characterize him as a merchant adventurer. He participated in settlement activities in Ireland, in colonization activities of the Virginia Company and the New England Company, as well as in his own failed attempt at colonization of Newfoundland.

In 1620, George Calvert began an eight-year campaign to establish a colony in Newfoundland. During this time, James I died, and Charles I became king. While attempting to maintain his struggling colony, in 1624 George Calvert announced his conversion to Catholicism. He had been born into a Roman Catholic family, but had been raised and educated as a Protestant. For religious reasons, Calvert refused to swear the oath of allegiance and supremacy to the king, and he resigned from the Privy Council. One indication of the favor George enjoyed in court was the king's bestowing on him the title of Baron of Baltimore with land in the county of Longford in Ireland.

By 1629, Calvert had determined by firsthand knowledge that the hostile conditions in Newfoundland made his colony of Avalon impossible. He wrote to Charles I,

> I have found by to deare bought experience which other men for their private interests always conceled from me, that from the middst of October to the middst of May there is a sadd face of wynter upon all this land.... Hereupon I have had strong temptations to leave all proceedings in plantations, and being much decayed in my strength, to retire myselfe to my former quiett; but my inclination carrying me naturally to these kynd of workes, and not knowing how better to employ the poore remaynder of my dayes, that with other good subjects to further the best I may the enlarging yo'r ma'ty's empire in this part of the world, I am determined to committ this place to fishermen that are able to encounter stormes and hard weather, and to remove myselfe with some 40 persons to yo'r ma'ty's dominion in Virginia...

Subsequently, Calvert sailed to the Chesapeake Bay to examine that area personally, and upon his return to England, used his still considerable influence in court to obtain land in the Americas for yet another colonial enterprise. His ultimate colonial success was the crafting of the charter for the Maryland colony, which his son, Cecil, would establish after his death.

Charles I must have understood and respected the religious convictions that prompted Calvert's refusal to swear the oaths, or perhaps he was impressed with Calvert's determination, because the king subsequently entertained George Calvert's petition for a colony in what would become Maryland. The royal charter for this land in America—land that was then part of Virginia— included terms that gave the Lords Baltimore great authority over all matters in their new colony. But George Calvert died before the charter for his Maryland Colony was finalized.

The Maryland Charter

Following the death of his father in 1632, Cecil Calvert applied himself to winning the charter for the new colony in America. The Privy Council approved, and on June 20, 1632, King Charles I applied his royal seals to the Charter for the "Mary Land" province and granted the province to Cecil Calvert, second Lord Baltimore. The charter specified the name Mary Land in honor of Charles I's Roman Catholic wife, Henrietta Maria, sister to the king of France. The charter provided Calvert essentially princely authority over this new province. However, it had not come without a political fight from the Virginia Company and other detractors of the Calverts.

The charter and the powers it granted the Calverts were so politically controversial in England that Cecil Calvert could never visit the colony. He remained in England throughout his life, working diligently to maintain the Calvert authority over the province.

His brother, Leonard, led the colonists to Maryland aboard the *Ark* and the *Dove*, setting sail on November 22, 1633, and arriving in the Potomac River in early March, 1634. On March 25, 1634, they celebrated mass on St. Clement's Island in the middle of the river. That date marks Maryland Day, the beginning of the new colony.

Among the powers granted to the Calverts as Proprietors of Maryland were: the ownership of all the land, which they could dispense to colonists willing to make substantial investments; the right to make laws to govern the colony, without the need for royal approval; the right to establish an army and wage war to defend their territory; the right to hold court and impose sentences including death; the right to bestow noble titles on colonists and to create manorial estates with full feudal authority and fealty.

A sometimes-overlooked provision of the charter established the right and duty of all "freemen" to engage in

the legislative process. The charter made these provisions for a democratic form of government by giving the Proprietary the responsibility to enact laws "of and with the **advice, assent and approbation of the free men**" of the colony.

This set the stage for the Colonial Assembly to play a major role in the direction of the new colony. This franchise, similar to that existing in the Virginia colony, was thus broader and more effective than the parliamentary process that existed in England at the time, and it anticipated the U. S.

Cecil Calvert, 2ⁿᵈ Lord Baltimore Daniel Mytens, the Elder portrait

Constitution that guaranteed all freemen the right to vote by 150 years.

Under this provision, Matthias de Sousa, a free man of African ancestry and passenger on the *Ark*, voted in the General Assembly of 1642.[1] This charter provision also

---

[1] A brief biography of Mathias de Sousa appears at the end of this chapter.

formed the basis for a woman, Margaret Brent[2], to demand the right to vote in 1648. The assembly refused her demand for suffrage, and it was not until the 20th century that an amendment to the U.S. Constitution gave women the right to vote. Similarly, African slaves could not vote until the abolition of slavery and emancipation laws provided that right to them.

The Maryland charter was a masterful piece of legal work and became a prototype that subsequent colonial entrepreneurs hoped to receive from the crown. However, a significant phrase was added to the Maryland colonial charter that put later Lords Baltimore in conflict with the crown—a requirement to establish the Anglican religion as the favored religious body in the colony. A direct quotation from the charter is in order here. The charter reads,

> ...*the Patronages and Advowsons of all churches which...hereafter shall happen to be built, together with license and faculty of erecting and founding churches, chapels and places of worship...**and of causing the same to be dedicated according to the ecclesiastical laws of our kingdom of England.***

The portion of the wording that has been emphasized has been interpreted to mean that the crown's intent was to ensure that the Anglican religion would be that which enjoyed official support in the colony just as it did in England; in other words, there would be a state religion, and it would be the Anglican religion.

Religious Freedom and Separation of Church and State

At some peril, Cecil and Leonard Calvert skirted the issue in the charter of a state religion; they must have been mindful of the thin ice they skated on. In England, as previously stated, Catholics were persecuted, and practice of their religion was conducted in secrecy. The Calverts resolved to establish their colony as a commercial success, of course, but also as a place where all religions could coexist without

---

[2] See Chapter 3 for a biography of Margaret Brent.

conflict. Cecil Calvert, mindful of the prevailing attitudes towards Catholics, exhorted his Catholic colonists to be discreet in their celebration of their liturgy to avoid religious conflict.

The Catholic colonists made up approximately one in four of the early settlers—thus they were a numerical as well as religious minority. The majority of the settlers who practiced a religion were undoubtedly Protestant. Consequently, Calvert advised the Catholics embarking on the *Ark* and the *Dove* as follows:

> *His Lordship requires the Governor and Commissioners that in their voyage to Mary Land they be very careful to preserve vanity and peace amongst all the passengers on Shippboard, and that they suffer no scandall nor offence to be given to any of the Protestants, whereby any just complaint may hereafter be made, by them, in Virginia or in England, and that for that end,* **they cause all Acts of Romane Catholique Religion to be done as privately as may be***, and that they instruct all the Romane Catholiques to be silent upon all occasions of discourse concerning matters of Religion; and that the said Governor and Commissioners treate the Protestants with as much mildness and favor as Justice will permit. And* **this to be observed at Land as well as at Sea***.*

Thus began the Calvert establishment of a colony founded on the principle of separation of religion from matters of state, and the attempt to guarantee the toleration of different (at least Christian) religions. Incidents in which Catholic colonists abused the religious rights of Protestants were dealt with harshly by the Proprietor and the Provincial Court. The historical record discloses more than one incident when a prominent Catholic landowner was fined approximately a quarter-year's income for interfering with the practice of religion by Protestants. One example will illustrate how serious the Calverts were about the principle of religious toleration. Thomas Gerard, owner of the *Manor of St. Clements*, had a Protestant wife and had built a chapel at his manor that was apparently used by both Protestants and Catholics. In

1641, Gerard was accused of locking the chapel and removing the books of the Protestants. The Assembly summoned him to face these charges and subsequently found guilty. They ordered him to open the chapel to the Protestants and restore their books; his penalty of 500 pounds of tobacco was to be given to the first Protestant minister to arrive in the Province.

Clearly, the Lords Baltimore and those they entrusted with power in the early days of the colony took the principle of religious toleration seriously. They obviously also took the principle of separation of church and state seriously as well since they avoided the issue of making the Anglican religion the official religion, and they went to great pains to ensure that no religion was favored in the early deliberations of the Colonial Assembly or the Provincial Court.

This matter of principle was commendable, but Calvert's motivation must have been, at least in part, simple common sense. The Calverts knew that Roman Catholics were a small minority of the population; they knew they were under a great deal of suspicion and beset by political pressures in England based both on their religion and their competition for colonial opportunities. Later in the 17th century, they were also beset by land disputes with the neighboring colonies of Virginia, Delaware, and Pennsylvania. They simply could not afford to let religious disputes interfere with their commercial ventures in the New World. Consequently, their strict adherence to the principles of toleration and separation of church and state were vital to their own freedom to practice their Roman Catholic faith, and to keep the commercial venture viable.

At St. Mary's City, legend has it that all religions shared the first structure where services were held. That was an existing Indian longhouse. Later, they built a wooden chapel on the land now known as the Chapel Field. It is believed that Protestants as well as Catholics worshiped in that chapel, although the historical record does not exist to confirm or refute that belief. During this period of the wooden chapel, as

Catholics and Protestants died in proportion to their population, and as there were instances of intermarriage between the faiths, it is highly likely that non-Catholics as well as Catholics were buried in what came to be called "the Chapel Field."

In 1667, in the Chapel Field, at a site which placed it in harmonious alignment with the State House of the same period, the Brick Chapel was erected by the Jesuit priests who had accompanied the colonists to Maryland to minister to the Roman Catholics among them and also to the "Savages, having no Knowledge of the Divine Being ..." These two dramatic, ceremonial buildings were separated at the extreme ends of the carefully planned Baroque city in a symbolism that was probably an intentional reflection of Lord Baltimore's commitment to the separation of church and state.

By the end of the 17th century, this great experiment in religious freedom and separation of church and state ended. In two earlier periods of religious conflict, first in the 1640s when Richard Ingle, a Puritan, seized control of the colony, and again during the Protestant Rebellion of the 1680s when the "Associators" took control, religious toleration was suspended. Political events in England under William and Mary and later monarchs led to the suppression of the Roman Catholic and "dissenting" Protestant religions, and the establishment of the Anglican religion as the state religion in the colonies, including Maryland.

In 1704, passage of the "Act to Prevent the Growth of Popery" permanently closed the Brick Chapel. This law, with subsequent modifications, forbade the public practice of the Roman Catholic religion. There probably some who believe that the Brick Chapel was taken from the Jesuits in a dramatic and hostile show of force by the Protestants, wielding torches and pitchforks no doubt. However, the actual events, well documented by historical records, are much different.

The colony was certainly rocked by the civil disturbances in England in the latter part of the 17th century, and school-children today hopefully know well the role played by Margaret Brent in maintaining the order of the colony in the absence of the Calvert leadership. But the acts which led to the abandonment of the Brick Chapel were lawful acts taken by the Colonial Assembly and the Royal Governor. These acts invoked the royal imperative quoted above from the charter, and put in place the establishment of the Anglican religion as the official religion of the colony. As onerous and as discriminatory as the acts are known to be today, they were enacted lawfully at the time.

The Jesuits determined that the celebration of the Catholic religion was therefore no longer possible in the Brick Chapel. Consequently, sometime after 1705, they made a conscious decision to dismantle the Brick Chapel and reused the bricks to build their manor house of *St. Inigoes*, south of St. Mary's City.

Catholics for a long period after that time had to celebrate their religion in secret in private homes. The acrimony between the Protestants and Catholics can be found in various public records, including the last will and testament of Thomas Loker, dated 1799, in which he left the following instruction with regard to his bequest to his daughters:

> ... *and in case of either of their intermarriages with a roman catholic, I then cut them off with one shilling sterling, and what I have within bequeathed them to be equally divided amongst the remainder of them* ...

Ultimately, other colonists took control of the Jesuits' Chapel Field lands through a re-patenting process, and the land became an agricultural field. The graves of Catholics and Protestants alike soon became indistinguishable under the plow. Whatever grave markers existed have been lost as well. Finally, archaeologists at Historic St. Mary's City relocated the site of the Brick Chapel and hundreds of graves, as well as traces of wooden structures, in the Chapel Field.

What we have learned is that the original settlement at St.

Mary's City, the first capital of Maryland, was not an enclave of Catholic zealots; it was a settlement founded on the principle of separation of church and state, where all the colonists were initially guaranteed the right to practice their religion freely. It was also the first site in the New World where a man of African descent voted as a member of an English parliamentary body—the General Assembly of Maryland.

Religious freedom, the right to vote and participate in the legislative process, regardless of race or religion, are high principles that did not exist in England, and which 150 years later were incorporated into the Bill of Rights of the United States of America. These high principles emanated from a pragmatic adventurer who was motivated as much by commercial success as by his religious beliefs.

He understood that Catholics, being a minority population persecuted in their home country of England, must ensure that they adhered strictly to the practice of toleration in order to succeed in this new colony. Later in the 17th century, the colony abandoned these important principles, and one of the symbols of the separation of church and state, the Brick Chapel, was dismantled by the Jesuits.

In 1696, Governor Francis Nicholson moved the capital to Annapolis, and from 1694 to 1828 the State House, the other symbol of the separation of church and state, served as an Anglican church. In 1720, the Colonial Assembly deeded to the Anglican parish the land and old State House. In 1829, Bricks from the state house were reused in the construction of the current Trinity Church on the old state house grounds.

Historic St. Mary's City Today

The mission of Historic St. Mary's City, the custodian and interpreter of the site of Maryland's first settlement, is to preserve, reconstruct, and interpret the important historical significance of the early days of Maryland. This 17th-century city has contributed greatly to the political fabric of our nation. Great events occurred in St. Mary's City that preceded the founding of the nation by more than 100 years. The lessons of the establishment of a colony based on the principle of separation of church and state, embodying the principle of tolerance and democratically directed governance, are a major part of the important story of Historic St. Mary's City.

For this reason, the Historic St. Mary's City Commission has begun reconstruction of the Brick Chapel in as faithful a representation as possible, using the materials and methods of the 17th century, and based on extensive research into extant examples of Jesuit churches of that period. The reconstructed Brick Chapel will be used by the Commission to demonstrate the principle of separation of church and state, a national cornerstone principle that started in St. Mary's City. The graves of the early Catholic and Protestant colonists in the Chapel field will be treated with the utmost respect. Lead coffins containing the remains of the Calvert family, discovered and excavated just a few years ago, will be re-interred with full honors in their original resting place once the reconstructed Brick Chapel is complete.

The Chapel, along with the reconstructed State House, will thus symbolize the contributions of Maryland to the cherished freedoms and human rights embodied in the United States Constitution.

Matthias De Sousa
First African American Legislator

Matthias De Sousa "Molato" is listed as a passenger on the *Ark* by Father Andrew White, the Jesuit chronicler of the first voyage to Maryland.[3] De Sousa probably boarded the *Ark* during its stop at Barbados in the West Indies prior to beginning the final leg of the voyage to the Chesapeake Bay. Father Copley, another priest in Maryland, listed De Sousa as one of the persons transported to Maryland by the Jesuits. The Maryland Archives record the following:

> *Matthias de Sousa made oath that about March (1641) was twelve month he was appointed by Mr. Pulton [Father Ferdinand Poulton] to goe in his pinace as skipper and trader to the Sequhanoughs and by him appointed to hire men at Kent for the voyage ...*

According to the Maryland Archives, Matthias De Sousa attended the Assembly of March 1641/1642. He had apparently completed his time of indenture or the Jesuits had freed him of his indenture, since only freemen could attend the Assembly. This gives Matthias De Sousa the distinction of being the first African American to vote in an English-speaking legislature. He later entered into an indenture with John Lewger for settlement of a debt.

The name De Sousa is Portuguese and there have been a number of notable De Sousas in the 16th and 17th century including:

Martim Alfonso De Sousa—a 16th-century Portuguese Admiral who commanded the first colonizing expedition to Brazil (1530-1533). He was later governor of the Portuguese colony of Goa in India.

Thomé De Sousa—a Portuguese nobleman and soldier of the 16th century who led a 1,000-man expedition to Brazil ca 1549. He was the first governor-general of the colony of Brazil.

---

[3] Given De Sousa's boarding the *Ark* in 1634, he could well be one of the earliest known African slaves in Barbados.

Luis De Sousa—a 16th and 17th-century monastic historian of the Dominican order.

It is interesting to speculate that Matthias De Sousa could have been a decedent of one of these men. It is plausible that the two military men would have spent time in the West Indies, and Thome' De Sousa had served in Africa and India prior to his campaign in Brazil. In addition, Africans were living in the West Indies by the 16th century, having been brought there as slaves by slave traders such as John Hawkins of England circa 1565.

Unfortunately, we know nothing else about Mathias de Sousa in Maryland. He may have died as an indentured servant, or could have regained his freedom before he died, but the record is silent on the remainder of his life.

Aleck Loker

Margaret Brent
Attorney, Adventurer, and Suffragist

Chapter 3
Margaret Brent
Attorney, Adventurer, and Suffragist

Three hundred and fifty-eight years ago, Margaret Brent appeared before the Maryland legislature demanding the right to vote. She owned, through her own business acumen, a substantial amount of land in Maryland and Virginia, and functioned as a highly competent attorney in civil law cases and at least one criminal case.

Who was this Englishwoman living in colonial America, and how could someone thought of at that time as a middle-aged "spinster" have had the temerity to take such a bold step? Unfortunately, Margaret Brent is hardly recognized in England or America for the great adventurer, attorney, and human rights pioneer that she was. It is high time that her English and American countrymen give her the honor and recognition that she deserves.

To understand what motivated Margaret Brent, we need to think about her world of the early 17th century in England, Europe, and America. We also need to know more about her—her family and how she may have been raised. This biography traces what we know about Margaret Brent's life in England and America, and offers some speculation on factors that may have affected her character.

Margaret Brent's Early Life and Education

Margaret was born around 1601, one of thirteen children of Richard Brent and Elizabeth Reed Brent of Gloucestershire in England. Her parents had six boys and seven girls.

We know little of the Brent children's education. However, one can infer that they were well educated for their time, perhaps by tutors and by education abroad. William, one of the younger children, attended to St. Omer's in the Low Countries for his education. The record shows that, by

1633, Laurence Lodowick[4], a Benedictine monk from Yorkshire, died at *Lark Stoke,* the Brent home. He may have been Richard Brent's chaplain and could have assisted with the education of some of the Brent children.

Lark Stoke Manor
The Brent home in England

Margaret and four of her sisters remained unmarried throughout their lives. Three of her sisters, Catherine, Elizabeth, and Eleanor, became nuns. The reason for Margaret's and Mary's decision to remain single is unknown. Although it we don't know whether Margaret and Mary (who accompanied her to America) traveled to the continent, Margaret certainly exhibited continental social attributes. At that time in England, women did not usually engage in

---

[4] Interestingly, Fulke Greville had a cousin, Lodowick, who was involved in a complex estate fraud and murder for which he was convicted. The Lodowicks may have been related to the Grevilles and the Brents.

serious intellectual discourse with men. In the Low Countries, to the contrary, women freely engaged in such dialog and generally enjoyed freer movement within society. We know that Margaret's three sisters were nuns at Cambrai (now part of France). It is conceivable that Margaret visited them there before coming to America.

Antonia Frazer, writing in *The Weaker Vessel,* has said, "Many of the daughters of the English Catholic families ... continued to be sent abroad to convents in the Low Countries to receive their education.... But these girls who wended their way to the Low Countries, often remaining there as nuns, also found a kind of independence unknown to their sisters still at home ..."

It is also conceivable that Margaret and Mary had been exposed to the proselytizing of Mary Ward, an Englishwoman from Yorkshire where the Calvert family lived. The Calverts—founders of the Maryland Colony— were cousins of the Brents. Mary Ward had joined the Poor Clare order on the continent and returned to England, leading a clandestine group of Catholic women. Her uncles (named Wright) were implicated in the infamous Gunpowder Plot.[5]

Mary Ward founded the English Poor Clares convent at Gravelines, France. Mary Clifton, Margaret Brent's niece, entered that convent. Thus, the Brents knew of Mary Ward, and Margaret and Mary Brent may have secretly joined Mary Ward's sect. However, no direct evidence of this has been uncovered.

The public record in Maryland discloses that, as an adult, Margaret was self-assertive in that exclusively male society. Her strength of character and obviously capable intellect, evident in her public life in Maryland, imply that Margaret

---

[5] The plotters felt that James I had not gone far enough to restore rights to Catholics, and, in November 1605, they attempted to blow up Westminster. The plot had the reverse effect of encouraging the Protestants to enforce more rigorously the recusancy law.

had received some formal education and had formed her strong, independent character before her decision to immigrate to America at the age of thirty-seven.

Suffering for Their Religion

Richard Brent's family converted to Catholicism in 1619 when his daughter, Catherine, decided to profess publicly her faith in that religion. It is noteworthy that George Calvert, the First Lord Baltimore, "converted" to Roman Catholicism in 1624 soon after Richard Brent's family. In the villages where the Brents were located, the "old" religion (Catholicism) was never fully eradicated. Henry VIII had officially established the Church of England and its supremacy ca. 1531. After Henry and the brief reign of his son, Edward VI, Queen Mary had attempted to reestablish the Catholic religion in England. It was not until the reign of Elizabeth I, starting in 1558, that there was a sustained attempt to root out Catholicism.

Consequently, by the time of the Brents' conversion, England had been resolutely opposed to Catholicism for only about sixty years—about two generations. Also, by the 1620s, King James I was conciliatory towards Catholics, particularly the Catholic rulers of Spain and France. His successor, Charles I who was married to a Catholic, continued this more tolerant time for English Catholics during Margaret Brent's early years.

John D. Krugler, noted scholar of this period of Roman Catholicism in England, has written of the first Lord Baltimore's return to the religion of his youth:

> ...in casting his destiny and his family's with Catholicism, George Calvert did not respond to some unconscious desire for martyrdom. To the contrary, in openly declaring their allegiance to the Catholicism, the Calverts joined a viable, rejuvenated community that had made the adjustments necessary to survive and was growing in number. By the 1620s, the existence of a Catholic community, numbering 50 and 60,000, was no longer in question. Catholicism

survived among a substantial number of the gentry and nobility both in the countryside and in London.

It may therefore be more probable that the Brents' and the Calverts' "conversions" were public acknowledgments of their true religious beliefs, which had been suppressed in the earlier years. It was true of the Calverts and the Brents in America that they practiced their religion in private and didn't attempt to convert their Anglican neighbors.

Children often feel more passion for religious or social causes than their parents. Parents have learned to temper their passions to get along in society, whereas their children have yet to learn that lesson. Such may have been the case in the Brent family where their religion was concerned. Richard may have been practicing peaceful coexistence with his Anglican neighbors, but his teenage daughters were unwilling to keep their true religious beliefs hidden. In any case, once they made the religious decision, the Brents' fortunes changed drastically.

Richard Brent paid heavily for his public profession of the Roman Catholic faith. After Margaret and several siblings had gone to America, two-thirds of *Lark Stoke Manor* was sequestered (seized). The property was seized because in August of 1644, during the English Civil War, Richard Brent had allowed Royalists to fortify his home at *Lark Stoke*. Parliamentarian forces ultimately overran the house and placed Brent under arrest, imprisoning him at *Warwick Castle*. A letter written at the time referred to one of Brent's co-conspirators, Richard Canning of *Foxcote*, as "a notorious and pestiferous Papist... [who had] betray[ed] some of the Compton Garrison into the enemies hands...." Taking part in this engagement were also Richard Brent's sons Edward and George. The letter writer referred to them as "arch-Papists." The Brents were ransomed—probably at great expense. This paints a picture of clear loyalties—Papists aligned with Charles I, and good churchmen of the Anglican religion aligned with Parliamentary forces.

However, the historical record is somewhat less clear. The Brent *Manor of Admington* had been purchased by Lord Brooke's executors. He was a cousin of Richard Brent's wife. Lady Brooke asserted that she bought "enclosures" in *Lark Stoke Manor* from Fulke Brent (presumably after Richard's death in 1652). Later in the century, *Lark Stoke Manor* would be back in the hands of Richard Brent's grandchild, Robert. Lady Brooke and her husband's executors had taken legal possession of the Brent property to preserve it for their Catholic relatives until such time as the English sequestration of Catholic property was repealed. The repeal occurred under Charles II in the 1660s and implied a degree of tolerance for Catholics.

What happened to Margaret's brother William is an even more graphic indicator of the heavy penalty paid by the Brents for their religious and political beliefs. William, after his education by the Jesuits at St. Omer, studied law and was admitted to practice as a barrister at Grey's Inn in 1641. That same year, suspected of playing a role in the Irish Rebellion, Parliament ordered William arrested and imprisoned him in the London Gatehouse. He was subsequently moved to the Tower of London. Although Charles I had been tolerant of Catholics and William had been officially posted to Ireland, by the 1640s the seeds of religious and political turmoil were sown. William eventually gained his release from prison and practiced as a barrister successfully for many years. He died in 1691, age eighty years.

Four Brent Children Decide to Go to Maryland

As you can see, the Brents of *Lark Stoke* were all too familiar with the suffering of English Roman Catholics— even the high-born, well-connected Catholics. The threat of persecution, particularly if they had joined a secret Catholic order of nuns, must have been a strong motivation for Margaret and Mary to take the adventurous step of emigration to Maryland.

Their brothers Giles and Fulke would have shared this motivation; also, they were probably motivated by the promise of land and wealth. Giles stood to inherit nothing in England. Fulke, while in line to inherit his father's estate, could probably see that it would be of little value due to the growing political pressure and the civil penalties, fines, and property sequestration imposed on recusant Catholics.

The Brents' Influential Contacts

Margaret Brent used her access to some of the most influential people in England to ensure that she would be treated as equal to other adventurers traveling to Maryland. She had Lord Baltimore, the proprietor of the colony who was her cousin, write letters of instruction to Maryland Governor Leonard Calvert giving Margaret and her sister Mary the same rights to land as free male colonists. This was critical to her and her sister since there was a possibility that their rights to land would be forfeit if they didn't marry once in the colony. This precaution by Margaret reinforces the idea that she and Mary may have joined a secret order of Catholic nuns and could not marry, putting them in jeopardy of losing their land in the Maryland colony without Baltimore's written assurance. The letter from Baltimore guaranteed that Margaret and Mary would enjoy the same property rights as male adventurers.[6]

---

[6] The Brents had important connections in court circles in England. In addition to dealing directly with Lord Baltimore, Margaret could have called on the influence of her cousins Sir Fulke Greville (Lord Brooke) and Nathaniel Brent, both of whom were well received in court. Furthermore, it is now known that Margaret Brent and Anne Arundel, wife of Cecil Calvert, Lord Baltimore, were cousins. They were, in fact, related in several ways, but the closest and most important appears to be their common relationship to Sir Robert Willoughby. In addition to being related to Margaret Brent and Anne Arundel Calvert, Sir Robert Willoughby at one time owned *Wardour Castle* and manor, the home of Sir Thomas Arundel, Anne's father, and the location of the house where Anne and Cecil Calvert lived. Sir Thomas's father bought the manor and castle from the Grevilles who had inherited title through Elizabeth

Margaret's important relatives enabled her to have access directly to a man of Lord Baltimore's status. We must also remember that Lord Baltimore was a promoter, selling his colonial project to English gentry. The Brents were just the kind of people he needed—Roman Catholic gentry with an economic incentive to take the risk of immigrating to Maryland. Consequently, Lord Baltimore would certainly have encouraged Margaret Brent's enthusiasm for the adventure.

Willoughby, wife of Fulke Greville. Sir Edward Greville was the guardian of Elizabeth Willoughby, one of the richest heiresses in England at that time. She had extensive land holdings in eight English counties, including *Wardour Castle* and manor.

Consequently, the common relationship between the Brents and Arundels through the Willoughby-Greville line would have been known to the Brents. It would have certainly been a point of pride for Margaret's maternal grandmother. This relationship between aristocratic cousins explains how Margaret Brent had direct access to Lord Baltimore at Wardour Castle.

The title history of Wardour Castle and manor would also have been known to the Arundels. Ownership of land and the provenance of property has always been information that has been passed down through the generations. The acquisition of *Wardour Castle* from the Grevilles of Warwickshire would have been an important tie between them and the Arundels, and by extension a connection to the Brents who were closely related and apparently under the protection of the Grevilles.

While the Brents' fortune was declining, they would have been even more mindful of their relationship to the wealthy and influential Grevilles. Fulke Greville bought and restored *Warwick Castle* at great expense. That former royal property was the most imposing estate in the region where Margaret lived. She could certainly have felt proud that her great-uncle had accomplished so much. That he had once owned *Wardour Castle* and had sold it to Sir Thomas Arundel's father also would have been a point of family pride.

Fulke Greville may have been responsible for Richard Brent's commission as sheriff. Later, as has been stated, Lady Brooke, widow of Fulke Greville, Jr., acquired some Brent lands and held them through the sequestration period, after which they returned to the Brents.

The Brents in Maryland

Therefore, Margaret and her three siblings started on their American adventure with good credentials and the confidence of Lord Baltimore. They traveled to the colony of Maryland on the ship *Elizabeth* out of London, arriving in Maryland on November 22, 1638. Mary, Giles, and Fulke accompanied Margaret. Soon after their arrival at St. Mary's City, Giles and Fulke Brent were appointed to the Governor's Council.

Margaret certainly demonstrated a strong conviction that women should play an equal role in Maryland society. She received the first proprietary land grant to any adventurer in St. Mary's City, the capitol of the colony, on October 7, 1639, the year after her arrival. Margaret and Mary established their own residence, which they called *Sisters' Freehold*.

Independent from their brothers, Margaret and Mary began to increase their fortunes. One of her contemporaries observed that "Margaret requires far more land than we can afford." This statement illustrates Margaret Brent's drive to succeed on her own terms and, perhaps, the annoyance of men in the colony that two apparently eligible unmarried women planned to remain blissfully unwed. At that time, there were about 400 men and very few women in Maryland.

The English Civil War's Effect on Maryland

In England, supporters of Parliament engaged in armed conflict with King Charles I and his allies. The Roundheads, as the Puritan Parliamentarians were called, took the conflict to Maryland when Richard Ingle, in his ship *The Reformation*, invaded St. Mary's City in February 1645. He attacked the fort and proceeded to plunder the dwellings and other buildings there. Ingle took Giles Brent prisoner and returned to England with him.[7]

---

[7] On February 14, 1645, Giles Brent was aboard the Dutch ship *Looking Glass* when it was captured by Captain Richard Ingle, sailing on *Reformation*. Giles, who had been acting governor the year before, had

During the upheaval caused by Ingle's invasion of the capitol, Margaret remained in St. Mary's City while the colonial governor, Leonard Calvert, fled to Virginia. Although written accounts are sketchy, Margaret maintained some semblance of order and must have served as an inspiration to those loyal colonists who endured harsh treatment at the hands of Ingle's men. She owned, along with her brother, a ship called *Phoenix* that Ingle seized during the first uprising. Margaret also lost a "cabonette" containing jewels worth fifty pounds, cattle, crops, and household utensils.

In Virginia, Governor Leonard Calvert, Lord Baltimore's brother, raised a small company of militia to cross the Potomac and regain control of Maryland. Warfare in England and America at that time was fought by a few professional soldiers who raised armies from among the populace. They commonly offered these citizen-soldiers plunder in lieu of pay. This was probably an attractive inducement, particularly to the more adventurous souls. Plunder offered immediate compensation, whereas regular pay might be slower in coming and could be of less value.

You can imagine that taking part in this sort of adventure had a natural attraction for brigands as well as the adventurous aristocracy in English society. Such was the case with the militia assembled by Governor Calvert. They came from Virginia with the expectation of plunder if they met with armed resistance at St. Mary's City. Calvert had promised to pay them if there was no resistance. He didn't wish to see his fellow colonists further abused if they welcomed the proprietor's agent back—they had suffered enough at the hands of Ingle. In fact, Ingle's depredations

---

arrested Ingle and thrown him in prison for making treasonous speeches against the king. Ingle mysteriously escaped, perhaps with help from the sheriff, and sailed back to England with a grudge against Giles Brent. Not surprisingly, when Ingle, on his way back to sack the Maryland colony, found Giles aboard a Dutch ship near St. Mary's City, he took him prisoner.

were so great the colonists referred to that period of rebellion as "the plundering times."

With a show of force by his militia, Calvert peacefully regained control of St. Mary's City in 1647. However, by June 9, 1647, Leonard Calvert was dying. Just hours before his death, he named Thomas Greene to succeed him as governor and designated Margaret Brent as executor of his estate. His instructions to her were to "take all and pay all." Aside from that very broad charge, he left little else in the way of instructions other than a few bequests of clothing and cattle.

After making his wishes known publicly, the dying governor dismissed everyone except Margaret. We don't know what they talked about in private; however, it's reasonable to assume that Calvert discussed his concerns about the colony, his children in England, and his trust that Margaret would protect all of them. In addition, it is not known whether he gave Margaret advice about tactics to use in dealing with the General Assembly, the court, or creditors, including the militia from Virginia who were owed their pay.

At the time of his death, Governor Leonard Calvert had two children less than four years of age: William and Anne. According to legend, their mother, purported to be Margaret Brent's youngest sister Anne, died following the birth of their daughter.[8] Whether Governor Calvert's wife was Margaret Brent's sister has never been verified by documentary evidence. Father Andrew White, a Jesuit priest at St. Mary's City, referred to Margaret and Mary as Leonard Calvert's "kinswomen"—implying some relationship, either by blood

---

[8] Leonard's marriage would have taken place in 1643 when he had returned to England. He remained there for more than a year, saw the birth of his son, and began the life of his daughter, whom he probably never saw. A baptismal record of Anne Brent, daughter of Richard Brent, Esq. of Admington, is recorded at St. Swithin in Quinton, on February 16, 1612, making her thirty-one years old when she would have married Leonard Calvert. Two child births in quick succession at her age may well have killed her. However, her marriage to Leonard Calvert is conjectural at best.

or by marriage. We know that Lord Baltimore had married Anne Arundel, cousin of Margaret and Mary. That may have been the extent of the relationship referred to by Father Andrew White.

Margaret Brent's Public Service

Leonard Calvert's appointment of Margaret as his executor left her with a substantial responsibility—one that would have challenged any skilled attorney. She had Calvert's estates to manage (extensive real property, personal property, servants, crops, and cattle), the interests of his orphaned children to consider, and the demands of the militiamen from Virginia.

Giles had not made matters any easier for Margaret. While Leonard Calvert was away in England, he had appointed Giles as acting Governor. By marrying Mary Kittamaquund, daughter of the emperor of the Piscattaway Indians (the supposed heir to the Indian lands in Maryland), Giles had managed to alienate Lord Baltimore. When Calvert returned from England, he found a number of problems related to Giles administration, not the least of which was Giles' marriage to the eleven-year-old Indian girl. Also during his absence, Margaret Brent had sued Leonard Calvert, as guardian for Mary Kittamaquund, to force the payment of a dowry upon his ward's marriage to Giles. Leonard Calvert must have seen Margaret's involvement in this as having been forced by her brother Giles.

So, in spite of these troubles created by Giles, Leonard Calvert had not lost confidence or trust in Margaret Brent since he gave her the responsibility to manage his affairs after his death. Clearly, he was able to distinguish between Giles' and Margaret's actions.

Maryland Secretary John Lewger apparently made Lord Baltimore back in England fully aware of Giles' activity. Because of Giles' behavior, Margaret would have to deal with a proprietor growing increasingly wary of the Brents.

The militiamen were also becoming impatient and threatening to take by plunder what Calvert had not paid them. On October 6, 1647, militia Captain John Price convinced the Provincial Court to issue an attachment of all of Calvert's estate in favor of the debt he asserted Calvert owed to the garrison of militia at St. Mary's City.

Margaret Brent approached Price's court action in a sophisticated legal way, proving her skills as an attorney. On December 13, 1647, presenting herself as Lord Baltimore's attorney (a role formerly held by Leonard Calvert), Margaret successfully sued a prominent planter named Thomas Gerard, Esq.[9] for his failure to pay the proprietor's duty on a tobacco shipment. The court accepted her as the legitimate attorney of Lord Baltimore.

She then arranged for the Provincial Court to formally recognize her as Leonard Calvert's executor and as Lord Baltimore's attorney. She apparently felt that both commissions were necessary to deal with the militia crisis. Since the issue of the garrison was related to Leonard Calvert's duties as Lord Baltimore's attorney (a responsibility apart from his governorship), she asserted as the deceased Calvert's executor that she should also assume his role as attorney for the proprietor until he made other arrangements.

Obviously, in that age before instantaneous trans-Atlantic communication, faxes, and Internet, the colony could not afford to wait months for ship-borne letters to resolve this matter. The court agreed and ratified Margaret Brent as

---

[9] Thomas Gerard was a doctor and member of the Governor's Council. He lived at *St. Clement's Manor*, which consisted of approximately 6,000 acres in 1642 and 11,400 acres in 1678. Gerard, a Roman Catholic, had been fined 500 pounds of tobacco in 1641 for preventing Protestant services in his private chapel—his wife was a Protestant. Dinner-time conversation must have been interesting in that household. Gerard would later be threatened with banishment and confiscation of his estates for his part in the Fendall Rebellion of 1660. Doctor Gerard was clearly a controversial individual for Margaret Brent to bring criminal charges against.

Leonard Calvert's executor and Lord Baltimore's attorney on January 3, 1648. This permitted her to use the deceased governor's or Lord Baltimore's assets to satisfy the demands of the militia and any other Calvert creditors. It also set the stage for the act for which she should be most famous—her petition for the right to vote.

Margaret Brent's Demand for the Right to Vote

You might ask why Margaret Brent took that next decisive step. She probably could have paid the militia with cattle and other property owned by the Calverts without further legal authority. However, she may have felt (and may have been instructed by Leonard Calvert on his deathbed) that the debt to the militia was a debt of the colony rather than a personal Calvert debt. On January 21, 1648, Margaret Brent attended the meeting of the General Assembly at *St. John's*, home of Secretary John Lewger, and demanded to be allowed to participate.

Specifically, she asked for "voice and vote"—full participation in the legislative process. She based her demand on her status as a freewoman, landowner, and as Lord Baltimore's attorney. Some believe she took this step because she wanted to persuade the Assembly to impose a public assessment to pay the militia, thus relieving herself of the need to use Lord Baltimore's or Leonard Calvert's assets to pay that debt. She may also have believed in the rightness of admitting women into this male domain. However, on that latter point, it is noteworthy that she had been a free woman landowner for nine years and had apparently not been motivated to demand voice or vote before.

Governor Greene refused Margaret Brent's demand to speak and to participate in the assembly. There is no record of the proceedings to tell us why he did so. It could have been because she was a free woman landowner—not a free man. The reason may have been more complicated than that.

Since the first session of the General Assembly in 1635, political tension existed between the Lord Proprietor and the colonists. The intent of George Calvert, First Lord Baltimore, and his son Cecil (as reflected in the Royal Charter that granted their dominion over Maryland) had been to establish a colony based on the principle of benevolent paternalism similar to English rule during the Tudor reign. Under the Tudor kings and queens, the Privy Council exercised great power and was an instrumentality of the crown. Parliament ratified the regal wishes expressed through the Privy Council. The proprietor planned and expected to establish the Maryland colony on similar political principles, and he expected to build fealty to his rule through the granting of manorial lands and titles.

However, the political climate was shifting in England. Parliament was becoming more independent, and in Maryland, the colonists exhibited similar independence. Much to Lord Baltimore's chagrin and annoyance, that first Maryland General Assembly of 1635 rejected the laws the proprietor had drafted and sent over for their ratification. During the intervening years, the General Assembly had held to what they saw as their right as freemen to exercise "local initiative." This tension continued throughout the colonial period. Giles Brent was implicated in an anti-proprietary plot in the Assembly, or at least so believed Lord Baltimore.

Governor Greene, presiding at the General Assembly of 1648, certainly knew of the issues surrounding Giles Brent, including the alleged anti-proprietary plot and his marriage to the Indian princess. There is no question that Giles had lost favor with the proprietor. In addition, Margaret, herself, had sued the proprietor's late brother for the Indian girl's dowry. Yet here was Margaret Brent demanding to take part in the legislative process as attorney representing Lord Baltimore. Her action presented Governor Greene with a dilemma. Could he give Margaret Brent voice and vote in those proceedings and run the risk that she would push the proprietor's agenda? Did he know she intended to introduce a proposal to tax colonists to pay the militia? Bear in mind, these colonists were reeling from the depredation of Ingle's rebels. They probably felt in no position to take on what they perceived as Lord Baltimore's personal financial obligation—a debt promised by his brother Leonard. Consequently, Greene faced a difficult situation: whether to allow a woman to sit in the legislature—one who presented herself as the proprietor's representative. Greene may also have felt that, as governor, he alone should be the representative of the proprietor.[10]

Greene took the most obvious, politic, and least troublesome course. He refused Margaret Brent's demands. Although she protested and attempted to disrupt the General Assembly, they continued to sit.

A number of historians may argue that Margaret Brent played an important role in saving the Maryland colony during the crisis following Ingle's invasion, but diminish her role with regard to human rights. They may say that Margaret Brent's motivation in demanding the right to vote in 1648 was merely on her own behalf or as Lord Baltimore's attorney.

Margaret Brent was bold enough to enter the male-only world of the Assembly and demand to be heard and vote, not only as Lord Baltimore's attorney, but also as a female land-owner. To apply the suffragist standards and definitions of the late 19th and 20th centuries to Margaret Brent's actions is an inappropriate test for a woman of the early 17th century.

---

[10] In time, the General Assembly would evolve into a bicameral body. By 1656, the upper house consisted of the Governor and the appointed councilors. The lower house was the elected burgesses. By 1722, the upper house, dominated by Governor Charles Calvert, was accused of being assistants to Lord Baltimore's prerogative, nullifying any offensive acts passed by the lower house. This legislative tension would continue until the Revolutionary War and the Constitution of Maryland. Some would say that the "local senatorial privilege" extended even today on "local matters" is a vestige of that proprietor's prerogative conflicting with local initiative.

Great social change usually comes about through a succession of personal acts of courage. We can analyze the actions of any single participant and, in the process, diminish their importance. However, the personal nature of the actions or statements give them impact. Patrick Henry is remembered for saying, "Give me liberty or give me death." A personal statement—not an abstraction. Martin Luther King talked about his "dream."

Rosa Parks rose one morning and went to the bus stop. She was black. She had been black all of her life and presumably had obeyed the segregationist civil restrictions imposed on her because of her blackness. But when the bus came that morning, she sat down and refused to give up her seat to a white person when told to do so by the driver. Whether she took her action on behalf of all African Americans, or because she felt personally affronted is, in the end, of little consequence. Her courageous personal stand made her a pioneer in the civil rights movement.

Similarly, we can speculate on what motivated Margaret Brent to summon the courage to enter the Assembly and demand two votes. She had been a woman all her nearly fifty years, and she had been a free landowner for nine. However, on that day, she said by her actions that she believed her sex was irrelevant when it came to the right to speak and participate in the legislature.

We will never know whether she took her action on behalf of all women. However, Margaret Brent was an intelligent and perceptive woman who could clearly see the future consequences of her actions. She understood the principle of setting precedents. While she may have decided to demand the vote because of her duty to Lord Baltimore, nonetheless, she surely understood that granting her—one woman—the right to vote would set a precedent for other women.

Consequently, the courage that Margaret Brent showed in demanding the right to vote for herself is certainly the first known instance of a woman demanding the right of suffrage in America. Most great social changes have come about from a series of smaller but important steps. Such was Margaret Brent's contribution to the field of woman's rights and, more broadly, human rights.

Undaunted by the Governor's refusal, Margaret applied herself to her duties to Leonard Calvert's estate and heirs and to Lord Baltimore. Her actions protected the estate ultimately inherited by Leonard's son, William. She also maintained order when the militia was near revolt by settling some of their claims for payment. She used cattle and property owned by the Calverts to satisfy the militia. The colony faced the very real prospect of plunder by the militia that under Leonard Calvert's leadership had saved them from the plunder and harsh treatment by Ingle's rebels. Margaret Brent's management of this crisis saw Maryland through very troubling times, and the colony's leaders would testify to that.

Lord Baltimore wrote a scathing letter to the General Assembly when he learned of Margaret Brent's disposition of some of his property. He expressed his suspicion of the Brents' motives and denounced Margaret Brent for her actions. However, the General Assembly clearly understood the importance of what Margaret had done and defended her in their reply to the proprietor, stating,

...as for Mrs. Brents undertaking and meddling with your Lordships Estate here...we do Verily Believe and in Conscience report that it was better for the Collonys safety at that time in her hands than in any mans else in the whole Province after your Brothers death...

Margaret Brent, Attorney

Much of the public record speaks to Margaret's inclination towards litigation to resolve problems. We can see by examining her ancestry and immediate family members that the Brents had a penchant for legal matters. Robert Brent, the late 15th-century progenitor of the Brents of *Lark Stoke*, is listed at St. Mary's Church in Warwick as having attained the degree of Doctor of Legal Letters. As previously mentioned, Margaret's brother, William, was a barrister of some prominence in London. Margaret's cousin, Nathaniel, was a highly respected barrister and educator at Oxford. Her father was sheriff of Gloucestershire and thus responsible for enforcing the laws.

Margaret must have grown up in a family in which discussions of the law occurred frequently. Even without formal training, she would have learned the basic principles of law in that environment. Several of Margaret's nephews went on to distinguished legal professions in England and America. Her brother Richard's son, Robert, became a very prominent barrister under Charles II and James II. Her brother George's sons, George and Robert, became prominent attorneys in Virginia as well as highly successful planters and politicians.

Therefore, it is not surprising that Margaret used the courts in Maryland so frequently and successfully on her behalf as well as for Leonard Calvert's heirs and other clients. Court records show Margaret Brent's name 134 times between 1642 and 1650. That level of legal activity clearly establishes Margaret Brent as a singularly independent woman with a penchant for public discourse. Her opponents in these cases were men, often of very high standing in the community, including the governor.

Aside from the number of civil law cases Margaret Brent took part in, what really distinguishes her as an attorney is that, acting as a prosecuting attorney, she brought criminal charges of contempt against Edward Commins who had defied an order of the Governor. The official record of this action reads as follows:

Nouembr 6 Mrs Margarett Brent, his Lps Attorney complayneth agst Edw: Commins, on behalfe of the Ld Propr of this prouince. ffor hauing in contempt of his Lps Authority & gouermt wittingly & knowingly taken certaine persons & goods under exequuon out of the Sheriffs hands. Vttering likewise att the same time words of great contempt agst his Lps Gouernor & the authority of the gouermt ffor wch fact of his the sd Attorney on his

69

Lps behalfe requyres tht the sd Edw: Commins may bee censured, & punished, as the Court shall find the fault to deserue.

She took this action in her capacity as Lord Baltimore's attorney, and the court found in favor of Lord Baltimore, fining Commins 2,500 pounds of tobacco. This marked the end of Margaret's tenure as Lord Baltimore's attorney. By February 9, 1649, she had made her last court appearance on his behalf

The Brents in Virginia

In April 1650, Margaret Brent gave power of attorney to "her loving friend" George Manners to act in Maryland on her behalf and for her brother Giles, and she and Mary moved to Virginia. By September 2, 1650, the Provincial Court asserted,

...Giles Brent has done or attempted to do divers things prejudicial to the right honble the Lo: Propry of this Province and his undoubted right and title thereunto and contrary to the trust reposed in him by his Lopp.

The court appointed George Manners to "...make dilligent inquisicion into this charge and prosecute him in the Provincial Court." This must have placed Mr. Manners in an untenable position. Apparently, he took the prudent step of doing nothing, as there is no further information about this case in the records.

Because of his difficulties with Lord Baltimore, Giles Brent had moved to Virginia sometime after 1648. Within three years, and possibly before, Giles had aligned himself with Governor Berkley of Virginia, and occupied land in northern Virginia— territory directly across the Potomac from Southern Maryland, claimed by both Maryland and Virginia.

Giles brought with him Mary Kittamaquund, who was then about twenty, and for whom he must have felt some affection. By that time the issue of her inheritance had been made clear—she was not heir to the Indian lands. Giles and Mary had two children: Giles II and Mary. Giles II was under twenty when his father died in 1671. The Brents settled on land between Potomac Creek and Aquia Creek in what is now Stafford County. They secured this land by headright[11] in Virginia. In 1651, Giles received patents for the land he had settled.

The Brents expanded their land holdings in Virginia substantially. Giles, Margaret, and Mary patented 10,752 acres between August 20, 1651 and March 29, 1666, greatly exceeding their land holdings in Maryland. While in Virginia, Margaret devised her headright for 1,000 acres to her nephew, James Clifton.[12] By will, she left her remaining headright in Maryland to her nephew, George Brent. The Brent name appears on various properties and landmarks in Virginia. At Aquia, Brent Point marks the mouth of Aquia Creek.

The Roman Catholic Brents had left a relatively safe haven for Catholics in Maryland in exchange for a politically safer haven in Virginia, or so it seems. Virginia had passed restrictive penal laws against Catholics in 1641. However, as

---

[11] Headrights were the method by which colonists were entitled to land based on the number of people they brought into the colony. The actual acquisition of land took three steps. The recognition of the headright based on the number and sex of people transported resulted in a warrant authorizing a surveyor to layout a tract of land. The surveyor returned a certificate with the metes and bounds on a plat authorizing application for a patent. The Governor then issued the patent, which conveyed fee simple title to the property. The practice was time consuming, and because currency was scarce, headrights were often traded not unlike trading marketable securities today. The only land in Maryland that Margaret and Mary actually took title to (other than as attorney for Leonard Calvert, etc.) was their 70 1/2 acre "Sisters' Freehold" in St. Mary's City. Margaret's acquisition of large tracts of land took place in Virginia.

[12] Records show that Margaret's niece Anne Brent, daughter of Richard of *Lark Stoke*, married James Clifton of Salwick, and they produced eight children including a son, James, and a daughter, Mary. The daughter of Anne Brent and James Clifton, Mary, was a nun in the order of Poor Clares at Gravelines.

in England of the 1650s, the laws seem to have been largely ignored in Virginia. The Brents probably practiced their religion in private, receiving services by visiting chaplains, as was the custom of wealthy Catholics in England.

Giles Brent not only acquired land, he also held military commissions and public office in Virginia. This would have been illegal under the strict enforcement of the laws against recusants. Governor Berkley and the Burgesses apparently turned a blind eye to the Brents' religion because of the strategic advantage the Brents offered them. In this early period of Brent occupation of the Northern Virginia, they were the northernmost English settlers in Virginia. They also occupied an area of land that, although on the western shore of the Potomac River, was claimed by Lord Baltimore. Giles Brent, with some military experience, and Margaret Brent's tenacious character made them excellent prospects to secure this area for Virginia.

The Brents were not cowering in the plantations they called *Peace* and *Retirement* in Virginia. During this time, Margaret and Giles witnessed William Bretton's second marriage to Temperance Jay at Newtown on Breton Bay in Maryland. Mary Brent also traveled to Maryland on occasion during this period. They continued to manage their business affairs in Maryland as well as Virginia, and in spite of Lord Baltimore's enmity, there is no indication that any attempt was made to inhibit their travels in Maryland.

Now they shifted their focus to their large holdings in Virginia. However, as late as 1661, Margaret Brent was involved in court actions in Maryland related to Leonard Calvert's estate. That same year Leonard's son and heir, William, came to live in Maryland at the estate called *Calvert's Rest*. He had to take legal action against Governor William Stone's widow, Verlinda Stone, to regain title to the *Governor's Field* property in St. Mary's City. William then married Elizabeth Stone, daughter of the Governor and Mrs. Stone— an interesting turn of events in his relationship with Verlinda.

Leonard Calvert's daughter, Ann, also came to Maryland where she married first Baker Brooke, second Henry Brent (nephew of Margaret, brother of George Brent), third Col. Richard Marsham, and fourth Judge Thomas Tasker. Brent relations with the Calverts must have improved at some point as evidenced by Ann Calvert's marriage to Henry Brent and by the burial of Jane Sewall Calvert, wife of the Third Lord Baltimore, in the Brent cemetery at Aquia, Virginia.

Margaret Brent, Businesswoman

Margaret amassed her fortune in Maryland and Virginia partially by taking title to Giles' patented lands and other property. More than once, Margaret came to Giles' rescue when his debts overwhelmed him. Giles found himself far more dependent on his sister than she on him. On October 18, 1642, she took title to Giles' holdings on Kent Island in payment for his debts to her and their uncle, Richard Reed in England. In Virginia on April 1, 1654, Giles Brent gave Margaret all his Virginia property including his shallop (boat), servants, and stock in consideration for her promise to support his wife Mary and to maintain and educate his children.

The conveyance of Giles' property to Margaret is further evidence of her financial success and his reliance and dependence on her. Soon thereafter, Mary Kittamaquund Brent died, still in her twenties. Around 1655, Giles married Frances Harrison, widow of Dr. Jeremy Harrison and daughter of Thomas Whitgreaves of Staffordshire, England. There was no issue from that marriage. Giles died circa 1671. His will was probated on February 15, 1672.

While he may have been an excellent military officer and perhaps an adept public official, Giles was equally adept at accumulating debt. Margaret became the business expert in the family. Some historians have wondered why Leonard Calvert made Margaret his executor rather than Giles. In light of Giles' dependence on Margaret in business matters, and Calvert's annoyance with the way Giles had served as Acting

Governor, it hardly seems surprising. Margaret had the foresight to secure land grants directly from Lord Baltimore before she left England. She moved quickly to establish herself independently in St. Mary's City, unwilling to depend on Giles or any other man. And she came to Giles' financial aid when he fell into debt. Who better for Governor Calvert to place his heirs' interest in than Margaret Brent?

The Brent Descendants

Giles Brent II, half English and half American Indian, had a short but successful life in Virginia. Although Roman Catholic and of mixed parentage, he was fully accepted into the Virginia society, serving as a commissioned military officer and collector of the tobacco taxes. He married his cousin Mary Brent, George Brent's sister, and they had several children. By May of 1679, Mary Brent had legally separated from Giles II, citing cruelty. Giles II died at his plantation in Middlesex County, Virginia, about three months later. He was twenty-seven years old.

Back in England, the Brent family had regained *Lark Stoke Manor* by the 1660s. Robert Brent, son of Richard and Margaret Peshall Brent, had inherited the property. Robert was a distinguished barrister and magistrate of Gloucestershire and Middlesex, very active during the reign of James II. He and his wife Catherine had a son and five daughters, four of whom were the last Brent residents of Lark Stoke: Elizabeth Conquest; Margaret Brent; Mary Brent; Dame Anne Lytcott; Frances Brent; and son, Falcatius Brent. All were Roman Catholic and nonjurors. Parliament issued an order to arrest Robert Brent in 1679, but he regained his freedom when the charges were dismissed. Robert later fled to the continent when James II was deposed. He died at Bath, September 20, 1694 of a fever "induced by drinking strong wine immediately after use of the hot baths."

Dame Anne Brent Lytcott was the last Brent to live at *Lark Stoke Manor.* In 1740, she died in poverty and was buried at St. Mary's the Virgin Church in Ilmington with her Brent relatives. The guide book to Warwickshire, "Hidden Warwickshire" by Betty Smith, has this to say about Dame Anne Brent Lytcott:

> *She seems to have been a formidable and somewhat lonely old lady, always known as "Madam," and she seems to have died virtually penniless, for the sexton records no funeral expenses for her, and all she left was a box of books of Catholic devotions.*

Like her great-aunt Margaret, Dame Lytcott must have been a strong-minded and independent person. Dame Anne's son, Robert Brent Lytcott, disposed of the estate after her death.

Margaret Brent's Legacy to the Nation

Margaret Brent died in Virginia in 1670. Her will, made on October 26, 1663, administered on May 10, 1671, left her property to Giles and her nephews and nieces. This pioneer left behind no children to carry on her spirit. However, her independence and strength germinated in America. Other women came after her clamoring for equality in society. But it wasn't until nearly 300 years later that women finally received the right of "voice and vote" in the American political process by the 19th amendment to the U.S. Constitution. She was a courageous and highly successful English settler in America, but she was above all a pioneer in the human rights movement and an active litigant on behalf of others.

Patrick Henry
The Spark That Ignited a Revolution

Chapter 4
Patrick Henry
The Spark That Ignited a Revolution

F
our distinguished but disheveled men stood outside the door of a small cabin in the mountains of Virginia. Dusting themselves off and stretching their cramped limbs, they were winded and sore from riding hard all morning to escape capture by the Green Dragoons under British Colonel Banastre Tarleton. All they wanted at this point was a warm place to hide, some home-cooked food and something to drink.

At their knock, the unpainted wooden door swung inward on squeaking hinges and a woman looked out apprehensively. "What do you want?"

"Pardon us, ma'am, we're looking for a place to rest for a short while on our way to Staunton. And we'd be most happy to pay you for some food and drink, and fodder for our horses."

"What are you doing here? Are you spies for them damned redcoats?"

"No, certainly not. We're running from them. They're trying to arrest us."

Thinking them Continental Army deserters, she said, "Cowardly dogs! Go away; I'll have nothing to do with you." She started to close the door in their faces.

One of the men waiting in the rear moved up to the front. "Ma'am, I'm Patrick Henry and these men are friends of mine from the General Assembly in Charlottesville. We just need a place to stay and rest for a while. Please let us come in."

"Patrick Henry, you say. Well, Mr. Henry is no coward. If you're him, you're welcome to come in and bring your friends with you."

Patrick Henry, Senator William Christian, John Tyler, and Benjamin Harrison (Speaker of the House) followed the woman into her cabin and avoided capture that day in June, 1781. To their hostess, as to most of the patriots throughout the western part of the Commonwealth of Virginia, Patrick Henry was a hero.

Patrick Henry made his reputation as a maverick, a bold orator who had the temerity to speak out against what he saw as unconstitutional treatment of the American colonies by the British Parliament and King George III. The common people of Virginia saw Patrick Henry as one of their own, a self-made man who had bettered himself by hard work rather than rising on inherited wealth and a rich son's education at the College of William and Mary. And they admired Henry's ability to express their views. He served first in the General Assembly and later in the Continental Congress. They knew they could rely on him to stand up to the aristocratic tidewater planters and even to the King of England to ensure the continuation of their rights.

On the other hand, the wealthy planters along the Chesapeake Bay and its tributaries at times mistrusted Henry, feared him, and were annoyed by his opposition to their policies, but they had to admire his power of persuasion. When he stood to speak to the assembly, they knew he could sway the majority to his cause.

Henry was a complex man, one who could be unpredictable and at times ambiguous, and one who is remembered in history more as a rabble-rouser than a statesman. However, many times during the lead-up to war with Britain and in the critical period of the formation of the United States of America, Henry provided effective and crucial leadership within the Commonwealth of Virginia and among the thirteen confederated colonies. This biography illustrates how Patrick Henry rose from humble beginnings on Virginia's frontier to achieve cult status as a ringleader in the call for independence and one who represented the conscience of the fledgling nation as it struggled to achieve a stable government of, by, and for the people.

Patrick Henry's Early Life

In 1716, Governor Spotswood led an expedition from Williamsburg over the mountains and into the Shenandoah Valley to secure the territory and open up the western areas for settlement by Virginians. When he and his men returned to Williamsburg, he created what he called the "Transmontane Order" and conferred on those who had accompanied him the title of "Knight of the Golden Horseshoe." The knights received a gold horseshoe in recognition of their accomplishment. In the years following the Governor's expedition, the population of Virginia expanded west and by 1740, had nearly tripled.

Among those western pioneers was John Henry, a Scottish immigrant to the colony, who had arrived in Virginia in February 1727. He came from a middle-class Aberdeen family and had enrolled in the university there but left without taking a degree. John Henry became a farmer in Hanover County living with Colonel John Syme, an acquaintance from Scotland, as a guest on his plantation called *Studley*. Syme died suddenly in 1731 and, within a year, his attractive widow, Sarah, married John Henry. She brought to the marriage one son, John Syme, Jr. Sarah came from the prominent Winston family and was heir to about 6,000 acres.

Sarah and John Henry had eleven children, four sons, and seven daughters. William was their oldest son and Patrick was the second. He was born May 29, 1736, and named for his uncle, Reverend Patrick Henry, Anglican minister at St. Paul's Church in Hanover County. Although John Henry held positions as Colonel in the militia, Chief Justice in Hanover County, county surveyor, church vestryman, and sheriff, he remained on the verge of bankruptcy throughout his life. He enjoyed fine whisky, gambling and dancing, and his speculation in land, farming, and other enterprises never prospered. As surveyor, he produced the first map of Virginia to include county boundaries in 1770.

Sarah became enthralled with the preaching of Presbyterian minister Samuel Davies. She looked with evangelical criticism on the way her husband led his life. Patrick Henry often accompanied his mother to the church to hear Reverend Davies preach, and there he learned the power of a dramatic style of oratory that used the full range of voice and body language to convey a powerful message.

Henry found he could master the preacher's style of speaking and would later put it to good use in his legal and legislative careers. He remained staunchly Anglican in his religious beliefs throughout his life. He learned technique and style from Reverend Davies but was not persuaded by his preaching.

However, he came to believe in the importance of religious liberty. In that regard, Reverend Davies may have influenced him as did his mother's interest in Presbyterianism. Henry would come to see that other faiths deserved full liberty, not just a grudging toleration or sufferance. His mother's disapproval of frivolity also influenced Patrick, and he never adopted his father's vices.

As a youth, Patrick Henry worked on his father's farm and, when not working, enjoyed hunting and camping in the forest, and playing the flute and the violin. When Patrick was thirteen, his half-brother, John Syme, Jr., came of age and took over *Studley* plantation. Patrick and his family moved to *Mount Brilliant* (also called *The Retreat*) about twenty miles away on the South Anna River.

While Patrick's father had taught him reading, writing, arithmetic, Latin and Greek, he had little inclination for more formal education. When he turned fifteen, he apprenticed for a few months to a merchant in Newcastle. Then his father borrowed money to set up Patrick and his older brother, William, in a small store. Within one year, they closed the store—a complete failure.

Two years later Patrick Henry announced to his family that he planned to marry his childhood friend Sarah (Sallie) Shelton. His parents were not enthusiastic about the marriage due to his and Sarah's youth. Sarah's parents shared the Henry's lack of enthusiasm, but both sets of parents stood with Patrick and Sarah in the front parlor of the Shelton home and Reverend Patrick Henry administered the wedding vows in October 1754. Their first child, Martha, called "Patsy," appeared early in the Summer of 1755—perhaps explaining why the Henrys and Sheltons reluctantly agreed to the marriage of eighteen-year-old Patrick and sixteen-year-old Sarah.

The young couple faced some trying times ahead. Patrick tried to make a go of farming *Pine Slash Farm*, Sarah's dowry, but in two years, he had achieved nothing. Their first summer, a drought destroyed their crops, and the second year their house burned. Patrick and Sarah moved into the tavern owned by the Sheltons, and Patrick tended bar and played the fiddle to entertain the customers.

In 1759, having lived and worked in the tavern for two years, Patrick Henry, age twenty-three, met Thomas Jefferson, age seventeen, at a Christmas party at the home of Colonel Nathaniel West. Jefferson told Henry he was on the way to begin his studies at the College of William and Mary in Williamsburg. Patrick had a different future before him and he didn't relish it: bartender and fiddler in his in-laws' tavern. He resolved to do better.

Soon after the Christmas season, he announced that he would become a lawyer. The profession of law required a prospective attorney to study and then submit to evaluation by lawyers designated to administer the examination. Henry, never one for lengthy studies, spent a short time listening to lawyers discuss their cases in the tavern, observed a few trials in the courthouse nearby, and read as much as he could stand of Edward Coke's treatise on English law.

That spring Henry traveled to Williamsburg to for examination by two eminent Virginia lawyers. He went first to George Wythe who was a friend of someone he knew in Hanover County. Wythe asked him a few questions and then endorsed his application. Then Henry crossed the palace green and rode the short distance to John Randolph's house where he endured a thorough interrogation lasting several hours. Randolph found Henry's scant knowledge of the law appalling but his intelligence and debating skills impressive. Randolph added his endorsement to Henry's application but admonished him to continue his studies of the law.

Patrick Henry stopped at Goochland Courthouse and tendered his application to practice law. He took the oath on April 15, 1760, and his fortunes soon took a turn for the better. His practice steadily increased as he took on clients in Hanover and the adjoining counties.

Henry's Rise to Political Prominence

After three years, the Louisa County Tax Collector hired Henry to represent him in what became a pivotal law case. The case evolved from a dispute between the Anglican ministers in Virginia and the local authorities. The Virginia assembly had passed the "Two Penny Act" that limited the amount of government funds customarily paid as an annual stipend to the ministers in each county. Parliament, in its role as overseer of colonial legislatures, had ruled that local act null and void, opening the way for ministers to sue to recover their full stipend in each county.

Reverend James Maury of Louisa County filed suit against his county tax collector to receive his full stipend and had the case heard in Hanover County before Patrick's father, Judge John Henry. Henry ruled in favor of the minister. He may have been less than impartial since his brother, Reverend Patrick Henry, had filed a similar suit against the Hanover County Tax Collector. For the phase of the trial to determine the amount of damages to award Reverend Maury, the Louisa Tax Collector hired Patrick Henry to represent him. He may have expected that Patrick could be persuasive with his father, the judge. Today, this blatant conflict of interest would not be permitted in court, but in those days, it was not uncommon.

Patrick Henry demonstrated his oratorical skill in defending the tax collector in the Maury case and argued that Parliament should have upheld the Two Penny Act. He said only a tyrant king would allow Parliament to overrule the colonial government. Maury's attorney accused Patrick Henry of treason for his remarks about the King and Parliament. When Judge Henry gave the case to the jury, they returned in five minutes with their verdict. Maury would receive one penny in damages. Evidence showed that he should have received £256. This case, referred to as the Parson's Cause, established two things: Patrick Henry had the ability to sway people to his cause through the power of his oratory; and Patrick Henry did not flinch from challenging the authority of the King and Parliament.

His defense of the prerogative of colonial assemblies to establish local laws to govern their citizens—a principle that he considered a compact between the king and his subjects—anticipated further challenges to royal authority by two years. In 1765, Louisa County selected Patrick Henry to fill a vacant seat in the House of Burgesses (the lower house of the Virginia General Assembly). The session of 1765 would launch the Virginia colony on the road to revolution.

Henry's Role in the Revolution

Henry arrived in Williamsburg as a new member of the House of Burgesses on May 20th. Nine days later, after a caucus with a small group of fellow delegates in the Ralegh Tavern, Henry introduced volatile resolutions protesting Parliament's imposition of the Stamp Act on the American colonies.

Under the act passed by Parliament on March 22, 1765, American colonists would have to pay a tax on every piece of printed paper they used. This included newspapers, legal documents such as wills and deeds, and papers filed as pleadings in court. The tax was small, but the principle was large since it represented a departure from the past in which the colonial legislatures, rather than Parliament, established their own tax levies. Patrick Henry's five resolutions are paraphrased as follows:

1. The first colonists brought with them all the rights and privileges of British subjects.

2. Two royal charters endorsed by King James I guaranteed those rights and privileges to the settlers of British colonies in America.

3. Taxation of the colonists must only be done by their own act and by people who are subject to the same taxes and able to judge their effect on the people. This principle is a distinguishing characteristic of British freedom and embodied in the ancient English constitution.

4. The colonists have uninterruptedly enjoyed the right to self-governance and the kings or people of Great Britain have not heretofore denied that right.

5. Any attempt to wrest this right from the people of the colonies will destroy British as well as American freedom.

Ralegh Tavern
Where Patrick Henry drafted the Stamp Act resolutions

His five resolutions articulated the right of the colonists to govern their own affairs and specifically asserted the principle that taxation without representation in the legislative body establishing the taxes was a violation of the British constitution—tyranny, in other words.

In this modern age, one could ask why it wouldn't have made sense to have colonial representatives sit in the British Parliament to adequately protect the colonists' interests. But in those days, communication between England and the colonies was difficult. Letters took months to travel across the Atlantic, and a representative from America would soon be out of touch with conditions in the colonies.

When Henry delivered his resolutions to the House of Burgesses, many showed shock and outrage. The Speaker of the House, John Robinson, charged Henry with treason—not the first time he had been so charged. Henry looked directly at the Speaker and said, "If this be treason, make the most of it." Or so the legend says. A written account by a Frenchman who witnessed the exchange that day in May indicates that Henry spoke a bit more contritely when charged with treason. He offered his apology to the House and said that his comments stemmed from to his interest in protecting his country's liberty and his passion may have moved him to say more than he intended.

But Henry's resolutions spoke volumes and would soon be public knowledge. The next day, the House of Burgesses adopted all five of his resolutions, but with a narrow margin in an assembly with only about one-third of the members present. On May 31st, the House attempted to expunge the fifth resolution from the record, but the newspapers had already printed all five resolutions. Because of these resolutions, Royal Governor Francis Fauquier dissolved the Virginia General Assembly on May 31, 1765.

Popular sentiment supported Henry on this issue as it would throughout the rest of his life. The newspapers included two additional resolutions that Henry and his caucus had drafted but had not presented to the House of Burgesses:

the sixth resolution asserted that Virginians should not obey any British tax law; and the seventh declared that anyone attempting to support Parliament's right to tax the colonists would be judged an enemy of Virginia. All seven of the resolutions made it into newspapers in Maryland and Rhode Island. Soon other colonies took up similar resolutions in their local assemblies and, in October, eight colonies convened a congress to oppose the Stamp Act.

Parliament would take measures over the next few years to affirm and enforce what they viewed as their supreme right to dictate to the colonial assemblies. And Patrick Henry, in his role as a member of the assembly, would resist all of Parliament's attempts, arguing that the colony had the right to self-rule. While some members of the House of Burgesses urged for conciliation with the crown, Henry said that the time for friendly overtures and submissive behavior was past. For ten years following the Stamp Act resolutions, various colonial governors would convene the General Assembly in Williamsburg, only to disband them after legislative acts the governors deemed treasonous. Patrick Henry was viewed as a ringleader in many of those acts.

By 1770, Lord North, the British Prime Minister, had formed a new government. He sent John Murray, the Earl of Dunmore to Virginia to serve as governor. He would have the distinction of being the last Royal Governor of Virginia. Dunmore attempted to limit the power of the General Assembly to enact local laws. In April 1773, Parliament passed the Tea Act, adding an additional tax on tea imported to the colonies. The Tea Act infuriated the colonies and strengthened their resolve to oppose Lord North's government and its attempt to impose such levies.

Patrick Henry played a principal role in opposing the British authority. George Mason paid tribute to Henry at that time, saying, "But his eloquence is the smallest part of his merit. He is, in my opinion, the first man upon this continent, as well in abilities as public virtue." However, not everybody viewed Henry as helpful. Some, who still hoped for a peaceful settlement of their differences with Lord North's government, viewed Henry as a rabble-rouser and a troublemaker—albeit a very effective one.

Henry and others drafted resolutions that resulted in the creation of a committee of correspondence to keep the General Assembly informed of actions taken by Parliament that might be injurious to the rights of the colonies. Governor Dunmore responded by dismissing the General Assembly.

In 1774, the colonies took the first steps toward self-government and called for the First Continental Congress. In August, Henry and his half-brother John Syme represented Hanover citizens at the Williamsburg Convention—called a convention because Governor Dunmore would not reconvene the General Assembly. The delegates to the convention agreed to a total boycott of British goods, and they appointed Peyton Randolph, Richard Henry Lee, George Washington, Richard Bland, Benjamin Harrison, Edmund Pendleton, and Patrick Henry to represent Virginia citizens at the First Continental Congress in Philadelphia in September.

The Continental Congress resolved to oppose the so-called "intolerable acts" passed by the government of Lord North, enacted the boycott of British goods, and refused to allow any public moneys raised in the colonies to be transferred to the crown. The intolerable acts included: a weakening of the authority of the Massachusetts government; an act requiring people charged with certain crimes in Massachusetts to be returned to England to stand trial; and a law requiring citizens to provide quarters to British soldiers in their privately owned dwellings.

More-conciliatory delegates to the Continental Congress wanted to send a letter to King George to entreat him, humbly, to redress the wrongs done by his Parliament. Patrick Henry, a member of the committee to draft the letter, wrote the first draft. He was soon replaced by someone with a more conciliatory temperament. The congress also drafted a Declaration of American Rights that insisted that Parliament had no authority over the colonies other than in matters of trade between the colonies and Great Britain.

When Henry returned from Philadelphia, he set to work organizing a militia in Hanover County. This was the first independent militia formed in Virginia. He clearly saw that Virginia and Great Britain were on a collision course, and he would do his part to prepare at least his part of Virginia to defend herself. Massed British troops in Boston made it clear to Henry that Britain planned to use armed force to bring the rebellious Americans in line and it would only be a matter of time, he thought, before redcoats arrived in Virginia.

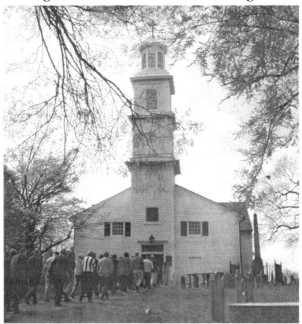

St. John's Church, Richmond

Patrick Henry's fervor reached a crescendo when the Second Virginia Convention convened in St. John's Church in Richmond on March 20, 1775. They met in Richmond instead of Williamsburg to ensure that Lord Dunmore would be unable to interfere with their assembly. Peyton Randolph, the elected Speaker of the Convention, offered a resolution to send a message to King George that the colonists respectfully asserted their rights to self-governance but repudiated forceful resistance to the crown.

That proposal prompted Henry to make the most famous and stirring speech of his life. He rose, looking earnest, with a grave expression on his angular face. He stood tall and, after a pause, began to speak. He spoke forcefully and passionately to the assembled delegates with all the skill and power he had learned years ago from Reverend Davies. After recounting the numerous aggressions of the British government towards the colonies, he proposed several resolutions calling for the establishment of a Virginia militia and other measures to put the colony in a state of defensive preparedness. Then he said, in part,

> *Gentlemen may cry peace, peace—but there is no peace. The war is actually begun! The next gale that sweeps the north will bring to our ears the clash of resounding arms. Our brethren are already in the field! Why stand we here idle? What is it the gentlemen wish? What would they have? Is life so dear, or peace so sweet, as to be purchased at the price of chains and slavery? Forbid it, almighty God! I know not what course others may take; but as for me...give me liberty or give me death!*

The stunned delegates took a moment to compose themselves and then adopted Henry's resolutions. They appointed him head of the committee to arm the colony. From that point forward, Henry would play a major role in the military defense of Virginia. The convention also moved to appoint the same seven men to represent the colony at the Second Continental Congress. Thomas Jefferson was appointed as an alternate for Peyton Randolph in case his health prevented him from traveling to Philadelphia.

On April 20th, Governor Dunmore ordered his marines to seize the gunpowder held in the magazine at Williamsburg. A similar move in Massachusetts had led to armed conflict, and there British General Gage failed to recover the gunpowder. What Gage failed to do by force, Dunmore accomplished by stealth. When the citizens learned of Dunmore's action, they were outraged. Patrick Henry heard of this in Hanover County, and on May 2, 1775, he announced his intention to march with the militia on Williamsburg to demand the return of the people's gunpowder.

The Powder Magazine in Williamsburg

Dunmore fanned the flames by saying that if the people moved against him, he would free all the slaves in Virginia who would take up arms in defense of British authority. Henry led his militia to Williamsburg in a two-pronged attack: one small force of a dozen men would seize the receiver general, Richard Corbin, at his home outside of Williamsburg; the rest of the force would surround the city to cut off Dunmore from escape—particularly to Yorktown. Henry made his headquarters a few miles west of the city.

Henry's plan began to unravel when the raiders on Corbin's house came back empty-handed. Corbin had spent the night in the city. The governor sent a messenger to Henry with an offer to pay £330 for the gunpowder he had seized. Henry hesitated at that point. Then Dunmore made a second major blunder: he declared that Patrick Henry was a traitor and called for his arrest. He also threatened to have the British warship *Fowey*, standing by in Yorktown, to fire on the town and destroy it. Thomas Nelson rode from Yorktown to Henry's camp at Duncastle's Tavern and said he would provide surety for Dunmore's payment for the gunpowder. Henry finally acquiesced and withdrew his militia back to Hanover County.

Henry left immediately to attend the convention in Philadelphia. Mindful of Dunmore's branding Henry as a traitor, militia along the way in Virginia and Maryland accompanied Henry to ensure his safe passage to Philadelphia. Had the British authorities arrested and convicted him as a traitor, he would have faced the following sentence: he would be hanged, but cut down before he had died; he would then be disemboweled, decapitated, and his body divided into four parts to be disposed of as directed by the king. But, he arrived intact in Philadelphia May 18, 1775, and supported the nomination of George Washington to assume the role of commander-in-chief of the Continental Army. From then on, Henry retired from the continental arena and devoted all of his energies to preserving Virginia's interests.

Henry's War Years

In August 1775, Patrick Henry assumed command of Virginia's newly established standing army, which consisted of two regiments of foot, sixteen battalions of minutemen and rifle companies, augmented by the county militia. Dunmore had fled from Williamsburg to a British ship at Yorktown on June 7th. This left a governmental vacuum filled by the Committee of Safety formed by the Virginia Convention. The Committee of Safety would provide executive oversight of the commonwealth until the formal establishment of a state constitution on June 29, 1776. During the interim, Henry moved his soldiers to Williamsburg and established an encampment behind the

College of William and Mary. He then applied himself to raising sufficient troops, material, and supplies to enable the Virginia military forces to defend the commonwealth.

Dunmore and his marines posed a real threat to Tidewater Virginia. The former royal governor remained aboard his ship offshore near Norfolk and sent raiding parties ashore to create as much havoc as they could. Colonel Woodford, led troops to Hampton to prevent its capture and destruction, while the rest of the troops under Henry remained at Williamsburg to keep the capital secure.

On February 13, 1776, the Continental Congress ordered the two Virginia regiments to become part of the Continental Army and offered Patrick Henry a commission under Brigadier General Howe. Henry declined this commission, preferring to remain in Virginia where he could continue to assist in the defense of the commonwealth. In May, the Virginia Convention reconvened and applied themselves to the prospect of separation from Great Britain. Henry used his leadership and eloquence to argue that Britain had ill-treated their colonies and that Virginians no longer owed allegiance to the king. He pushed to establish a union of the American colonies—one that would be totally independent of British authority. He called for a declaration of independence by the Virginia Convention. Edmund Pendleton offered a compromise resolution in which the Virginia delegates to the next Continental Congress would be instructed to introduce a declaration of independence for ratification by all the colonies.

Pendleton's resolution passed unanimously on May 15, 1776. When the citizens of Williamsburg learned of the passage of the resolution, they lowered the Union Jack and raised a continental flag over the capitol. The Virginia Convention now took up the business of forming an independent government, and they started with drafting a Declaration of Rights, which they approved on June 12th. Henry took particular pains to ensure that these rights included a strict adherence to religious liberty for all men.

Their document later served as a template for the U. S. Bill of Rights.

In the new government, a House of Delegates replaced the House of Burgesses, and a Senate took the place of the royal governor's Council. An elected governor would be the chief executive of the new government in the Commonwealth of Virginia. Patrick Henry became the first governor of the new commonwealth, elected by the members of the Virginia Convention now empanelled as the General Assembly (House of Delegates and Senate) on June 29, 1776.

He would serve three consecutive one-year terms, being replaced by Thomas Jefferson as governor in July 1779. During his tenure, Henry governed the most populous state in the union. He devoted most of his energy to the continual demands for troops, war materials and supplies needed desperately by the Continental Army, but he also involved himself in diplomacy, working through Benjamin Franklin to enlist support of the French for Virginia's war efforts. Henry also launched military efforts under George Rogers Clark in the western regions. As a result, Clark captured Kaskasia (now part of the state of Illinois) in July 1778, and then Fort Vincennes (now in Indiana) in February 1779. Those actions helped secure the western regions from incursions by British and Indian raiders, and strengthened Virginia's claim on those lands.

Soon after Jefferson became governor, he moved the capital to Richmond, and Henry enjoyed a short retirement from government. But he was back in the legislature by May, 1780. Henry supported Thomas Jefferson in his second election to the governorship, June 1780. Six months later, General Benedict Arnold sailed up the James River with 1,200 men bent on capturing the rebel leaders in Richmond. He captured Richmond and very nearly succeeded in capturing Thomas Jefferson, Patrick Henry and other Virginia leaders. However, they relocated to Charlottesville and reconvened; and when men under Arnold's command rode to Charlottesville, the General Assembly moved to Staunton and continued to conduct the business of the commonwealth there.

The war had finally come to Virginia in earnest by the summer of 1781. British General Cornwallis, moving up the coast from North Carolina, would soon encounter French General Lafayette and General George Washington's Continental Army at the final confrontation at Yorktown. By October 19, 1781, the war officially ended with Cornwallis' surrender. As in most wars, however, fighting continued for some time in other areas, as news of the capitulation took some time to spread.

Henry during the Post-War Period

During the final stages of the war, a rift developed between Patrick Henry and Thomas Jefferson that would put those two patriots at odds for the rest of their lives. An inquiry launched by the General Assembly to examine Thomas Jefferson's conduct during his time as governor greatly disturbed him. Although the motion to conduct the inquiry came from George Nicholas, seconded by Archibald Cary, Jefferson thought Patrick Henry had influenced those men to enter the motion.

The motion evolved from allegations that Jefferson had not adequately defended Virginia from the invading British forces. From that time, Jefferson considered Henry to be his political enemy, and the previous cordiality between them ended. Jefferson referred to Henry in colorful phrases including "[He is] all tongue without either head or heart."

In other respects, Henry and Jefferson held similar views. Following the war, the fledgling country needed to establish itself on a firm financial footing internally and internationally. The Continental Congress needed to pay off huge war debts and depended on requisitions of funds from each of the colonies to meet those national obligations. Some colonies failed to meet the demands placed on them, and the Congress had little recourse to force the issue. Between 1781 and 1786, the requisitions from the states had not even yielded enough funds to service the interest on the foreign debt. Patrick Henry was elected to two more terms as Virginia Governor in 1784 and 1785, and, during his tenure, Virginia prospered, generally meeting its financial obligations and even accumulating a surplus in the public treasury. The mounting foreign debt and other issues led to the question of whether a stronger federal authority should be created to have the power to levy taxes directly on the citizens of each of the states.

Both Henry and Jefferson believed in the wisdom of limiting the federal authority. Both men also saw expansion west beyond the Blue Ridge Mountains as crucial for the security and prosperity of the new nation. Both men would work to see that goal accomplished.

Henry had always advocated the sovereignty of the individual colonies. He strongly believed in the supremacy of states' rights. The form of government during the war years and immediately thereafter was a confederacy of states, bound together in their desire to gain their independence, led by mutual consent through the Continental Congress. But the individual states had not relinquished authority to the congress for most matters that would be important in peacetime such as taxation, interstate commerce and judicial matters. Had the situation not changed, the area now known as the United States of America would have functioned, if it survived, more like Europe before the European Union—an assembly of independent nation-states.

Henry was very wary of ceding any authority to a federal government. He found himself opposed in this regard by many Virginians he admired such as George Washington. On September 17, 1787, the Constitutional Convention approved a new U. S. Constitution and sent it to the states for ratification. This constitution would truly unite all the states under a strong federal authority, limiting the authority of the individual states. It needed nine states' approval to become the law of the land.

In Virginia, as in other states, the Federalists pushed hard for ratification of the constitution. Henry opposed ratification of the constitution. In addition to granting broad powers to a new federal government, the constitution lacked a clear expression of the rights of individuals. Henry learned that George Mason, Benjamin Harrison, and Richard Henry Lee, among others, shared his concerns. In June 1788, Virginia held a Constitutional Convention to consider ratification of the new federal government.

By that time, eight states had already ratified the constitution. Virginia, New York, North Carolina, Rhode Island, and New Hampshire had not done so. The debate in Virginia raged on for three weeks and centered on whether a Bill of Rights should be developed and added to the U. S. Constitution before the states voted to approve it. Henry clearly favored that approach, but eventually he had to concede that it was too late for all the remaining states to hold out. Approval would happen with or without Virginia

Finally, on June 25, 1788, Virginia ratified the U. S. Constitution in a very close vote—89 to 79. The ratification motion contained the caveat that the U. S. Congress would agree to consider amendments to the constitution that would insert a bill of rights offered by the Virginia delegation. George Wythe was the author of this motion, and he, along with Patrick Henry, George Mason, and Edmund Randolph, formed the committee to draft the bill of rights. The committee made little change to Henry's original draft of twenty constitutional amendments in the final bill of rights it presented to the Virginia Constitutional Convention.

Unbeknownst to the Virginia convention delegates, New Hampshire had ratified the constitution four days before Virginia, making that state the critical ninth vote. However, the bill of rights drafted by Henry and approved by the Virginia Constitutional Convention would be instrumental in the final drafting of the U. S. Bill of Rights.

Henry biographer Robert D. Meade observed that

It may well be argued, however, that no one had done as much as Henry to secure their [Bill of Rights] adoption. Without the pressure from him and his party, first in the Virginia Convention and then in Congress, it is doubtful if the United States would have had a federal Bill of Rights in its present form.

Patrick Henry in old age

After the convention of 1788, Henry resumed his practice of law full-time and worked hard to eliminate the personal debt he had incurred while in office. During these last years of his law career, he occasionally collaborated with John Marshall who would go on to become Chief Justice of the Supreme Court. George Washington, while he was America's first president, had offered the chief justice position as well as other federal positions to Patrick Henry. Henry declined each offer for federal service diplomatically— he had no interest in public service beyond the confines of his beloved Virginia. He also continued to invest in lands in Kentucky and other western territories. In September 1794, he retired from the practice of law.

Finally, George Washington convinced Henry to run once more for the House of Delegates. He easily won election in March 1799, but died at his home, *Red Hill*, on June 6, 1799, one week after his 63rd birthday. He never served in that session of the legislature.

Henry left a sizeable estate of thousands of acres in Virginia and in the frontier areas of western North Carolina and Kentucky. He had greatly exceeded his father in wealth, reputation, and public service.

Patrick Henry's Family

Henry was married twice. By his first wife, Sarah Shelton, he had six children: Martha (Patsy), John, Anne, Elizabeth, William, Edward (Neddy). Sarah died after Christmas 1774. She had suffered from mental illness for several years and toward the end had to be confined in one room under the care of one of Henry's slaves. Her death weighed heavily on Henry, and he went to the Virginia Convention in Richmond to deliver his famous "liberty or death" speech with her loss still fresh in his mind. In October 1777, while governor, Henry married Dorothea (Dolly) Dandridge, daughter of Colonel West Dandridge. Dolly was Martha Washington's first cousin. Dolly had turned down navy Captain John Paul Jones to marry Patrick Henry. He moved her and his extensive family into the Governor's Palace in Williamsburg. In an ironic twist, Patrick's son, John, had also been in love with Dolly Dandridge. Patrick and Dolly had eleven children: Dorothea, Sarah, Martha Catherine, Patrick, Fayette, Alexander Spotswood (named for Dolly's grandfather the former royal governor), Nathaniel, Richard, Jane, Edward Winston, John.

The Henry family lived in twelve residences in the 45 years of his married life. Other than the years in the Governor's Palace, they lived in modest homes seldom equal to the elegant tidewater plantation homes of Henry's aristocratic critics. Although personally restrained, Henry delighted in seeing his family enjoy themselves; he often played music as they sang and danced. He was known as a good, doting father who provided well for his family.

His Legacy

Patrick Henry is remembered as a rabble-rouser who challenged the wealthy aristocracy of Tidewater Virginia and sparked the American Revolution. He also protected Virginia's interests throughout his political career, contributed mightily to the war effort and the post-war development of

Virginia—at that time the most populous state in the union. He fought for the sovereignty of the commonwealth, in fact for all states' sovereignty, and when it became clear that the Federalist's vision of a new, strong central government would prevail, he fought to ensure that the new constitution would provide protection for the rights of individual citizens.

Less well known, Patrick Henry fought for religious liberty throughout his life. Although an Anglican, he acted on behalf of the "dissenting" religions in court, the legislature, and the governor's mansion to ensure the free exercise of other religious beliefs. Henry also upheld the rights and championed the causes of the hard-working farmers, merchants, and settlers, who his more aristocratic colleagues shunned. In protecting the interests of the western settlers, Henry enhanced their security from hostile Indians and British forces, and ensured that the Mississippi River was accessible to them. Some in the federal government, notably John Jay, would have entered into a treaty with Spain that would deny access to Americans on or beyond the Mississippi. Henry argued tirelessly to prevent ratification of that treaty. American expansion into the western territories formerly held by the British, French and Indians came in part through Henry's foresight and personal efforts.

Far from being just the spark that ignited a revolution against Great Britain, Henry played a prominent role in the war effort and the post-war development of the United States of America. He was one of the architects that transformed the American political landscape and moved the country from the colonial period into the modern era.

Aleck Loker

George Wythe
Venerable Statesman, Jurist, and Educator

Chapter 5
George Wythe
Venerable Statesman, Jurist, and Educator

A n old man lay dying in his home on Shockoe Hill in Richmond. His body had been wracked by agonizing cramps for two weeks. It was an unjust end for a man known throughout the Commonwealth of Virginia, in fact known throughout the new nation, as a paragon of virtue, a model of ethical deportment among attorneys, a guiding influence through the American Revolution and the subsequent development of the United States government.

This pathetic scene came about from the basest of emotions—greed and ingratitude—in this case the emotions of the old man's namesake and great-nephew. The teenage boy badly abused the trust and affection of his great-uncle by poisoning his morning coffee the day after he learned from the old man's will that he was his principal heir but would have to share part of the estate with a young black man.

The grand old man brought to such an inglorious end was George Wythe: teacher, attorney, distinguished jurist, and mentor of many of Virginia's finest statesmen. His alleged murderer was George Wythe Sweeney, grandson of Wythe's sister. As we examine George Wythe's illustrious life, we will learn how he impacted in a positive way so many Americans, making his untimely death all the more tragic.

Early Life
George Wythe was born in Elizabeth City County, Virginia in 1726 to Thomas Wythe III and his wife Margaret Walker Wythe. Thomas III died three years later, a relatively young man about thirty-four years old.
Thomas I, and Thomas II, George's great-grandfather and grandfather, also died young.

The Wythes came to Virginia from Norfolk, England about 1680. Thomas Wythe I, Gentleman, achieved some prominence in Elizabeth City County, serving as justice of the peace and member of the House of Burgesses. Thomas II also served as justice of the peace and as a trustee of the town of Hampton, but survived his father by only four months. Thomas III continued the tradition by representing Elizabeth City County in the House of Burgesses, served as a local magistrate, and added to the wealth accumulated by the two previous generations. He was a planter and half-owner of a wharf in Hampton, the principal port in Virginia at that time. He lived at *Chesterville,* an estate that is now part of the Langley Research Center in Hampton. Elizabeth City County has been absorbed by the City of Hampton.

Thomas and Margaret Wythe had three children: Thomas IV, Anne, and George. When George's father died, the bulk of his estate passed to George's elder brother. George received several slaves and some personal effects as his inheritance. He was an infant at that time. Margaret Wythe chose to educate George at home rather than send him to the Syms Free School nearby. Margaret, daughter of a prominent Hampton Quaker, had been well educated, and she taught George Latin and Greek as well as mathematics, logic, and grammar. She instilled in her young son a Quaker respect for all mankind, a love for the classics, for logic, and science that would distinguish him throughout his long life. He must have inherited from his mother a strong constitution because he greatly exceeded the lives of his paternal ancestors and could have lived much longer had not a murderer ended his life.

When George Wythe turned fourteen, he attended the grammar school at William and Mary. Two years later, he chose a career: attorney. He had two likely paths to pursue in following such a career. He could go to London and study at one of the Inns of Court, or he could remain in America and read law as an apprentice to a licensed attorney. George chose the latter path. His uncle, Stephen Dewey, who was married to Margaret Wythe's sister, had his law office in Charles City

County. George went there and began his studies. He spent two years under his uncle's tutelage and then returned to *Chesterville* where he continued his studies on his own. While there, his mother died.

When he felt he had sufficiently prepared, George rode to Williamsburg and presented himself for the examination and admittance to the bar. His examiners were Peyton Randolph, Saint Lawrence Burford, William Nimmo, and George's uncle Stephen Dewey. George Wythe passed easily and received his license to practice law on June 18, 1746. He was twenty.

Since his brother settled at *Chesterville,* George moved to Spotsylvania County where he could begin his law practice and live independently. He received his license to practice law in Spotsylvania County in November 1746. George lived with Zachary Lewis, the King's Attorney in that county. Lewis needed someone to help with his caseload, and George came highly recommended. Soon George took an interest in Zachary Lewis' daughter, Ann. Their marriage license was issued on December 26, 1747. The Lewis family had clearly welcomed George Wythe into their hearts, and he must have looked forward to many pleasant and rewarding years among them.

But, in little more than seven months, Ann had contracted a fever and died. George Wythe was bereft at her loss. He later wrote that he drowned his sorrow in the inns of Spotsylvania County. If so, he soon put that behind him because he had relocated to Williamsburg by October 1748— three months after his wife's death. He joined Ann's uncle, Benjamin Waller, in his law practice in Williamsburg and the surrounding counties.

A Fresh Start

At that time, Williamsburg was a thriving, if small, town of 1,000 to 2,000 residents. When the General Assembly convened in April and October, the town population more than doubled, with visitors attending the legislative sessions and participating in the horse races and auctions that occurred at the same time. Wythe saw that a law practice in the capital city of the Virginia colony would afford him more opportunities; he could make a fresh start. The proximity of the College of William and Mary was also no doubt attractive to Wythe, whose keen interest in the classics, philosophy, and science remained as strong as ever. Here he could enjoy the stimulating company of like-minded academics.

Reconstructed Colonial Williamsburg Capitol of 1705

The government of Virginia at that time was vested in a resident governor who received instructions from the Privy Council and the Board of Trade in London. The power of the governor extended to the right to appoint all but the lowest public officials and militia officers. He received advice from a council composed of twelve members appointed by the crown for life. Those council members invariably came from the loyal landed gentry that took the place of nobility in the colony. The governor had veto power over legislation passed by the General Assembly composed of the House of Burgesses and the Council. And he could prorogue or dissolve the General Assembly whenever he felt they had overstepped their bounds.

Besides embarking on his law career, on October 28, 1748, George Wythe was selected to serve as the clerk of two important standing committees in the House of Burgesses: the Privileges and Elections Committee, and the Propositions and Grievances Committee. This was his first step in a long political career. He was probably helped along by Benjamin Waller and by the contacts Wythe had already made in the House of Burgesses, including his uncle, and men such as Peyton Randolph, who had examined his mastery of the law just two years before. His duties as clerk consisted of taking and presenting the minutes of the committee meetings.

George Wythe, as a young and unproven attorney in Williamsburg, would have had stiff competition from men such as John and Peyton Randolph, Robert Carter Nicholas, and later Edmund Pendleton. However, within a few years, George Wythe had secured some very important clients including John Blair, an attorney himself and great-nephew of Reverend James Blair (the founder and first president of the College of William and Mary), Henry Fitzhugh of King George County, and the prominent Custis family of New Kent County. (Martha Dandridge Custis, widow, would marry Wythe's good friend George Washington in 1759.) Wythe added Robert Carter to his distinguished list of wealthy clients within a few years.

Wythe brought a strict sense of integrity to the practice of law. He insisted that his clients tell him the truth. If he found that they failed to do so, he would return their fees and refuse to represent them. In a profession not always noted for taking the high moral ground, George Wythe behaved in a way that was beyond reproach. His adherence to the strictest ethical standard added to his reputation and eventually led him to an outstanding career as a jurist and a law professor. Reverend Lee Massey went so far as to call George Wythe "the only honest lawyer I ever knew."

Beginning of a Political Career

Resident Governor Robert Dinwiddie had received permission from the London-based Board of Trade to charge a fee for applying his signature to land grants in Virginia. Virginia had been without a resident governor for a couple of years and, by 1751, Dinwiddie knew that a large backlog of land grants awaited his signature to make them legal. He was authorized to charge one pistole (nearly £1 then, about $240 today) as his fee for signing each land grant, the customary fee in other colonies but unheard of in Virginia. The House of Burgesses protested that the governor had not consulted with them or the Council about this fee and felt it should not apply. In 1752, the House passed a resolution stating, "Whoever shall hereafter pay pistole, as a Fee to the Governor, for Use of the Seal to Patents for Lands, shall be deemed a Betrayer of the Rights and Privileges of the People." The House dispatched Peyton Randolph, who served as the King's Attorney, to London to argue against Governor Dinwiddie's fee. Randolph sailed in December 1753, without the governor's permission.

Angered, Dinwiddie accused Randolph of abandoning his post and appointed George Wythe in January 1754 to serve as the King's Attorney—a rapid rise for this young attorney plucked from the midst of so many renowned lawyers in Williamsburg. George Wythe held the legal opinion that the governor had the right to charge the fee for endorsing the land grants—an unpopular opinion, but one that Wythe felt was legally correct. Wythe's appointment to Randolph's position, however, put him in an awkward situation as a usurper of one of the most popular men in the colony.

Later in August 1754, when Williamsburg's legislative representative Armistead Burwell died, the House of Burgesses selected George Wythe to fill the vacancy. This began Wythe's long career as a member of the legislature. Wythe assured the members of the House that he would resign his post as King's Attorney as soon as Randolph returned from England.

Wythe soon found himself embroiled in another political tussle. This occurred when the House of Burgesses appropriated £20,000 to support Colonel George Washington's campaign in the French and Indian War. In doing so, they stipulated that the expenditures would be subject to the oversight of a House committee. Governor Robert Dinwiddie, who had already dispatched Washington to the Ohio Valley to oppose the French there, felt the House of Burgesses had no right to review how he spent appropriated funds. He bristled at their impertinence. His friend George Wythe was a member of the committee of oversight. Throughout his life, Wythe would occupy such difficult positions and prove himself able to broker reasonable compromises.

Peyton Randolph returned from England in 1755, having received an agreement that the governor's authority regarding taxation would be limited and that Randolph could resume his duties as King's Attorney. That same year Thomas Wythe IV died and George inherited not only the estate of *Chesterville* but also his brother's position on the Elizabeth City County court—a position traditionally held by the Wythes.

Wythe's fortunes were now accumulating, and as an eligible widower, he courted the young daughter of a prominent Williamsburg man, Richard Taliaferro. George's medium build, blue eyes, high forehead and arched brows, along with his solemn and serious demeanor, must have impressed Taliaferro's daughter. Elizabeth Taliaferro lived at the family plantation, *Powhatan*, about five miles outside the city in James City County. She and George were married in 1755. Richard Taliaferro, a wealthy landowner and architect, designed and built a small estate for his daughter and new son-in-law in the city. The handsome brick house, prominently placed between Bruton Parish Church and the Governor's Palace, would serve as the Wythe home for more than thirty years.

George Wythe's Home on the Palace Green in Williamsburg

With Wythe's new duties as husband, busy attorney, and master of *Chesterville*, he neglected campaigning and failed to win election to the House of Burgesses from Elizabeth City County in 1756 and again in 1758. However, in 1758, the faculty of the College of William and Mary chose him to represent the college in the House—a position formerly held by Peyton Randolph, who had won election as a Williamsburg Burgess. Wythe served as the representative of the College of William and Mary in the House of Burgesses until 1761, when he successfully ran in the election for Elizabeth City County.

From Prominent Citizen of Williamsburg to Rebel

In 1758, Governor Francis Fauquier replaced Governor Dinwiddie. Fauquier was an intellectual with a broad range of interests including science (a member of the Royal Society), music, classical literature, philosophy, gambling and fine dining. He and his neighbor, George Wythe, soon forged a strong bond. They formed a small social circle that included Professor William Small from the College of William and Mary. Small, the only layman on the college faculty at that time, was professor of natural philosophy (science). Beginning in 1760, Thomas Jefferson, a young student at the college, became a regular participant in the dinners and discussions held by Wythe, the governor and Professor Small.

During this time, George Wythe established himself as one of the leading figures in the city of Williamsburg as well as the House of Burgesses. Wythe's powers of persuasion and negotiation frequently came into play as he took House bills to the Council for their consideration and concurrence.

One bill Wythe didn't support was the so-called Two Penny Act that temporarily limited the compensation for Anglican ministers in Virginia. Anglican ministers were due an annual payment of 16,000 pounds of tobacco. The crop shortage at that time inflated the value to about six pennies per pound. The Virginia General Assembly was considering legislation limiting the ministers' payments to one-third of the current price of tobacco.

Although Wythe opposed the bill—he represented the faculty of the College of William and Mary at the time, nearly all of whom were ordained clergy—but he failed to influence his fellow burgesses or the governor. When the Two Penny Act became law, Reverend John Camm took the clergy's case before the Board of Trade in London and they found in favor of the ministers. On August 10, 1759, the king disallowed the Two Penny Act and reprimanded Fauquier for signing it. Camm was back in Virginia in 1760 with the official decree. This precipitated a number of lawsuits in the county courts brought by the Anglican clergy to have their full annual stipends restored.

Colonial Williamsburg Courthouse

In Elizabeth City County in 1763, George Wythe sat as the judge in the case brought by Reverend Thomas Warrington. Wythe guided the jury through the legal arguments and to their conclusion, which was in favor of the minister. However, Wythe overruled the jury. This at first seems surprising since he had opposed the Two Penny Act and had argued in favor of the clergy receiving their full compensation when the act was before the House of Burgesses. However, his response to the jury in this case illustrates an important facet of George Wythe's character: he would invariably come down on the side of the law as he interpreted it. In this case, he felt that the General Assembly had acted within their purview and the governor had signed the Two Penny Act into law in keeping with the English constitution, as Wythe understood it. Therefore, he saw the Two Penny Act as the law of Virginia and argued that the crown had no business meddling in Virginia's local laws. Wythe's position coincided with Patrick Henry's position with regard to the Two Penny Act, although they arrived at their positions from markedly different perspectives. Wythe reached his conclusion from a logical and dispassionate analysis of the law as he saw it. Henry arrived at his position from his innate and passionate belief in the rights of citizens to govern their own affairs. It is noteworthy that Wythe took this position in opposition to the king thirteen years before the Declaration of Independence.

A year later, Wythe, as a member of the Committee of Correspondence, reviewed a letter from Edward Montague, Virginia's agent in London. Montague had forwarded the introduction of the infamous Stamp Act in Parliament.

The members of the committee were: John Blair, President of the Governor's Council; William Nelson, council member; Thomas Nelson, Secretary of State; Robert Carter, council member; John Robinson, Speaker of the House; Peyton Randolph, King's Attorney; Robert Carter Nicholas, member of the House of Burgesses; Lewis Burwell, member of the House of Burgesses; and George Wythe. After reviewing the letter from Montague and deliberation, the committee drafted the following resolution

> *Ordered that Mr. Montague be informed that this Colony is much alarmed at the attempt in Parliament to lay a duty on the sev[eral] commodities men[tioned] in their Votes, a copy of which he sent to ye com[mittee] particularly on Madeira wine & the proposal for a stamp duty. That he is desired to oppose this with all his influence & as far as he may venture to insist on the* **injustice of laying any duties on us & particularly taxing the internal trade of the colonies, without their consent.**

Thus began the argument against "taxation without representation." George Wythe and Robert Carter Nicholas drafted the letter to Edward Montague on July 28, 1764. The House of Burgesses took up the Stamp Act issue in November of that year. The Committee of Correspondence proposed four resolutions calling for the drafting of an appeal directly to the king; a memo to the House of Lords requesting reconsideration; an admonition to the House of Commons; and a letter to the Massachusetts House of Representatives indicating their accord with that body over their opposition to the Stamp Act. Wythe composed the letter of admonition to the House of Commons. His letter was so strident that many members of the House of Burgesses could not accept it. He was clearly not among the most conservative or conciliatory members of the House.

His letter read in part:

They [the Council and the Burgesses] *conceive it is essential to British liberty, the laws imposing taxes on people, ought not to be made without the consent of representatives chosen by themselves, who, at the same time that they are acquainted with the circumstances of their constituents, sustain a portion of the burden laid on them.*

Wythe's letter, with alterations to make it acceptable to the House of Burgesses, made its way to London, but the House of Commons refused to have it entered into their deliberations. They passed the Stamp Act on March 8, 1765. Wythe and the other members of the General Assembly learned of the Common's action in May. A large number of the assembly left Williamsburg at that time, willing to wait and see what came next from Parliament.

On May 30, 1765, only 39 of the 116 burgesses remained in town. Patrick Henry, a new member from Louisa County, proposed five incendiary resolutions denouncing the Stamp Act. Although his resolutions were similar to the correspondence sent to London only months before, Richard Bland, Peyton Randolph, and George Wythe opposed Henry. Their reason for doing so was that the resolutions added nothing new, and they felt that the points had been expressed in a more conciliatory tone in the previous correspondence to Parliament and the king. They argued that the previous correspondence had not yet been answered directly. They felt the House should wait a bit longer. Of course, the demeanor of the brash young man from Louisa County may also have put them off.

In spite of Wythe's and others' opposition, Patrick Henry's resolutions were passed and quickly appeared in the newspapers. Wythe and others moved to have the resolutions expunged from the record of the House of Burgesses, but the effort failed. Wythe clearly had not abandoned hope that the power of persuasion could be successful in the colonial dispute with the British king and Parliament. He didn't disagree with Patrick Henry in principle but only in the method to redress the unconstitutional position that they both believed Parliament had taken with the Stamp Act. Governor Fauquier quickly dissolved the General Assembly, viewing their resolutions as insubordinate.

Wythe still enjoyed the admiration of Governor Fauquier, and when Speaker Robinson died, Peyton Randolph resigned as King's Attorney so that he could become Speaker of the House of Burgesses. Fauquier nominated his friend George Wythe to the King's Attorney position. Wythe wrote to Benjamin Franklin in London to have him lobby on behalf of his appointment to King's Attorney.

However, Wythe's efforts were unsuccessful. John Randolph, Peyton's brother, became King's Attorney. John Randolph's loyalty to the crown had won him the plum position.

In 1768, George Wythe became mayor of the City of Williamsburg, an indication of his growing stature and popularity within the town. Also that year, Governor Fauquier died—a loss that George Wythe felt more than most Virginians. Fauquier had generally taken the side of the Virginians, to the extent that he could, in their disagreements with Parliament. His replacement, Norborne Berkeley, who had the title Lord Botetourt, would prove to be popular, but within two years, he died. A stern opponent of the colonial citizens, John Murray, the Earl of Dunmore, followed Lord Botetourt. Dunmore would remain as governor until the outbreak of the American Revolution.

Wythe clashed with Lord Dunmore early in his tenure when, sitting as the judge of the General Court, the governor refused to delay a case in which George Wythe and Robert Carter Nicholas were to be opposed by Edmund Pendleton and his missing associate. Lord Dunmore said, "Go on, Mr. Pendleton. You'll be a match for both of them." Wythe angrily replied, "With your Lordship's assistance!" Dunmore turned red and glared at Wythe. Wythe never enjoyed the close relationship with Lord Dunmore that he had experienced with governors Fauquier and Botetourt.

Wythe was now clearly on a collision course with those who would attempt to maintain London's control of the colonies. He had always been a strict adherent to the law and a well-read student of not only English common law but also classical democracy. He had taken his argument about self-governance from the philosophy of John Locke. He would find, as the next few years played out, that he could no longer support the king and Parliament.

Wythe's Role in the Revolution

During the period starting with the Townsend Act of 1767 up to the blockade of Boston Harbor in 1774, Wythe held the opinion that Parliament had no legal right to meddle with colonial internal trade or internal government within the colonies. He believed Virginia (and by extension, each of the other colonies) should be treated as an independent government giving allegiance to England's king or queen. Wythe had become one of the radicals who believed in the colonies' rights to self-governance. By 1774, Wythe held a position on the Williamsburg Committee of Safety along with Peyton Randolph, Robert Carter Nicholas, and Benjamin Waller. That committee would wield executive authority over Virginia during the Revolution.

Wythe was as outraged as the rest of the public when he learned that Lord Dunmore had secretly seized the arms and powder from the magazine in Williamsburg. He exchanged his well-tailored but somber frock coat for a rough hunting shirt, grabbed a musket, and marched in the military parade through the city. By June 1775, Dunmore had fled the city and boarded HMS Fowey, never to return to his seat as governor. Wythe, accompanied by Elizabeth, traveled to Philadelphia for the Continental Congress in August 1775. Their route took them across the York River on Gooch's Ferry through Hobb's Hole (Tappahannock) and Port Royal, then by ferry across the Rappahannock and Potomac Rivers, through Baltimore, Wilmington and Chester. Philadelphia was the largest of the colonial cities at that time, with about 30,000 residents.

Wythe's friend Peyton Randolph chaired the Continental Congress. King George III had declared the colonies in a state of rebellion, and Wythe, as well as all the other delegates, was considered a ringleader in the rebellion. However, there were moderates as well as radicals within the Congress. Wythe's stand became clear as he argued for establishment of free trade among the colonies. He said, "Turn your eyes to Concord, Lexington, Charleston, Bristol, New York. There you see the character of Ministry and Parliament." Those cities, of course, had already experienced violence and repression by British troops dispatched to restore compliance within the colonies. Wythe had concluded that the colonies needed to establish sources for goods independent of England, and they needed a navy to protect their rights to trade outside of England.

While George and Elizabeth Wythe were in Philadelphia, their friend John Randolph had taken his family to England demonstrating his opposition to the stand taken by his brother Peyton and all the others among the Virginia delegation at the Congress. Peyton Randolph died in October of 1775 while still in Philadelphia.

During the winter of 1775-1776, Wythe continued as a member of the Congress. Elizabeth was back in Williamsburg. Wythe continued to press for the establishment of treaties with other nations. He asked the other delegates, "In what character shall we treat? As subjects of Great

Britain? As rebels? Why should we be so fond of calling ourselves dutiful subjects? We must declare ourselves a free people." He called George III the "author of our miseries." By this time there could be no doubt that Wythe had abandoned any hope of changing Parliament's approach to the colonies through petition or conciliation. He recognized that the colonies would have to declare their independence from the mother country.

On June 7, 1776, Richard Henry Lee from Virginia offered a motion that the colonies formally declare their independence from Great Britain. John Adams of Massachusetts seconded the motion. However, the question was postponed until July 1st to allow the delegations an opportunity to get the concurrence of their respective assemblies. Meanwhile, Wythe's protégé, Thomas Jefferson, was selected to draft the declaration. Lee and Wythe left Philadelphia to return to Williamsburg. Wythe had in his possession Thomas Jefferson's plan for the government of Virginia as a free and independent state.

When Wythe attended the Virginia Convention and offered Jefferson's plan for the delegates' consideration, they found it too liberal. Among some of the more controversial aspects were Jefferson's language providing for separation from the Church of England, manumission of the slaves, free education for all, and broader voting rights.

By the time Wythe returned to Philadelphia, the Declaration of Independence, written by Thomas Jefferson, with amendments by Franklin and Adams, had been signed by most of the delegates to the Continental Congress. Wythe added his signature in September 1776, writing it above the names of the other Virginia delegates. By doing so, he left no doubt that he wanted to be seen as a leader in the movement to separate from Great Britain.

One of his final accomplishments that session was to move the Continental Congress to appoint Thomas Jefferson, Benjamin Franklin, and Silas Deane as the colonial agents in France—the first ambassadors of what would become the

United States of America. However, Thomas Jefferson and his wife had moved in with Elizabeth Wythe in Williamsburg. Jefferson stayed in Virginia rather than traveling to France due to his wife's ill health. His interest in crafting the new Virginia government also may have influenced his decision. Jefferson pushed a bill through the Virginia Assembly to amend the new commonwealth constitution. With George Wythe's return, Jefferson saw to it that Wythe would participate in re-drafting the Virginia laws along with Edmund Pendleton, George Mason, Thomas Ludwell Lee, and himself.

By March of 1777, Thomas Ludwell Lee had died; and Pendleton had fallen from his horse, his injuries preventing his attendance in committee. George Mason, tired of the tedious process, deferred to Jefferson and Wythe, who now had a free hand to finish the amendments to the Virginia Constitution as they saw fit. Soon, George Wythe was elected Speaker of the Virginia House of Delegates and assisted Governor Patrick Henry in ensuring that Virginia met its obligations to the Continental Army's war effort.

During his tenure, he also saw the changes to the Virginia Constitution passed in the General Assembly. One notable provision of the new constitution created the Chancery Court and the General Court system. George Wythe and Robert Carter Nicholas became the Chancery Court Justices. The Chancery Court at that time was the highest-level court in the commonwealth.

During the war, while the government moved to Richmond in 1780, Wythe maintained his home in Williamsburg. He remained there due to his loyalty to the college and the city, even though he was more exposed to possible capture there. Had he been captured by the British, he could have been returned to London for trial as a traitor. If found guilty, he would have been hanged, drawn, and quartered. In June 1781, General Charles Cornwallis came to Williamsburg and found the college closed due to a lack of students—they had enlisted in the Continental Army in time for the final battle at Yorktown.

It is not clear where George and Elizabeth Wythe were when Cornwallis came to the city, but one apocryphal story tells that Wythe and some companions were hunting at the mouth of College Creek when they came upon an advance party of British marines attempting to land there. Supposedly, Wythe and his friends opened fire on the British with their muskets loaded with birdshot. The British returned to their ship. About the same time, George Washington stayed in the city with George and Elizabeth Wythe prior to marching to his headquarters at Yorktown and his ultimate defeat of Cornwallis' forces.

Following the war, Wythe devoted much of his time to the process of converting a confederation of independent states into the new union of states as one nation under a strong federal government. Wythe took the side of the Federalists in his concept of how the United States of America should function. He went to Philadelphia to assist James Madison at the Federal Convention, but had to return to Williamsburg before they made any real progress. Although only 48-years old, Elizabeth Wythe was critically ill. George Wythe sent his resignation to Philadelphia and remained by his wife's side. She died August 18, 1787.

Wythe represented Williamsburg in the subsequent Virginia Convention to ratify the new U. S. Constitution. In the summer of 1788, he served as Chairman of the Committee of the Whole, guiding discussion and debate by all the members of the convention. His legal rival, Edmund Pendleton, served as President of the Convention. Wythe and Pendleton ensured that the strong opposition by Patrick Henry and George Mason did not derail Virginia's ratification of the constitution. Wythe used his skills to develop a compromise that broke the opposition's resolve: Virginia would approve the constitution, recognizing that it had significant faults, and would draft proposed amendments for consideration in the new U. S. Congress to rectify those faults. The compromise worked and the proposed amendments are substantially reflected in the U. S. Bill of Rights ultimately adopted by Congress in New York in 1789 and finally ratified by the states in 1791.

Educator

During the years leading up to the revolution, George Wythe worked as a plantation owner, a politician, and an attorney, activities which added to his growing wealth; but the activity that surely gave him the greatest sense of accomplishment was his role as a teacher. In 1760, Thomas Jefferson had come to Williamsburg, a seventeen-year-old student at the College of William and Mary. Soon, Jefferson became a private student living with and studying under George Wythe. During this arrangement, which lasted for about five years, the two men formed a lifelong bond of affection and mutual respect.

Wythe taught Jefferson to love the classics in Latin and Greek, tutored him in the law, history, science, and mathematics. Jefferson also emulated other personal habits and beliefs of George Wythe. Wythe ate sparingly, eventually adopting a nearly exclusive vegetarian diet, and drank wine moderately. He took a cold shower bath every morning, even in winter, and adhered to a rigid schedule of work and studies. Wythe's Quaker background influenced him in his belief of fair treatment for Indians and African slaves. In their beliefs concerning slavery, he and Jefferson were both conflicted. They personally abhorred the practice of slavery but could not conceive of a successful strategy to abolish it completely. Wythe and Jefferson also shared a lifelong interest in applied science. They both believed in religious liberty, freedom of speech, and government by the consent of the governed.

Jefferson's time under Wythe's wing exposed him to a number of contrasts that helped him develop his character: abstemious Wythe versus gourmand Governor Fauquier; Wythe's measured and, at times, tedious lecturing in court or the legislature versus Patrick Henry's fiery and sometimes overwrought oratory; Wythe's conservative but carefully tailored clothing versus the flamboyant manner of dress of many of his contemporaries. During his studies with Wythe, Jefferson certainly observed how highly regarded Wythe was for his strict code of ethics and his insistence on adherence to the fundamental rights of the citizenry.

Wythe sought truth and logic in the world around him. He applied those tests in the practice of law, in his participation in the government, and in his relationships with others. Jefferson shared and, perhaps, adopted those traits from his mentor. At times, Wythe could seem aloof and dispassionate, particularly when compared to more flamboyant figures such as Patrick Henry. He could also display a temper, particularly when nettled in the courtroom by his frequently successful opponent, Edmund Pendleton.

**The Wren Building, first academic structure
at the College of William and Mary in Virginia**

Wythe would take in other students, such as St. George Tucker in Williamsburg, and later, young Henry Clay in Richmond. Clay eventually went on to become the highly successful Kentucky representative in Congress, founder of the Whig party and, a man noted for his ability to broker a successful compromise, earning him the epithet "The Great Compromiser." He learned the power of compromise from his mentor, George Wythe.

When Thomas Jefferson succeeded Patrick Henry as governor in 1779, he, along with James Madison, President of the College of William and Mary, introduced a number of reforms in the college. One in particular, the creation of a new Chair of Law and Police, established the first college law curriculum in America. Not surprisingly, they appointed George Wythe to be the first Professor of Law and Police at the College of William and Mary. There were eighty students at the college that year. They paid 1,000 pounds of tobacco as their fee and could attend lectures by two professors of their choosing.

Wythe's salary as a professor at the College of William and Mary was eight hogsheads (about 8,000 pounds) of tobacco. He set about creating a course of law studies that was unique, and features of his method of teaching continue to this day in law schools throughout the country. Wythe held classes in the Wren building and moot courts in the old Capitol building in Williamsburg. He also had his students participate in mock legislative sessions to gain experience in parliamentary procedures as well as debate. He stated that his goal was "to form such characters as may be fit to succeed those which have been ornamental and useful in the national councils of America." In other words he planned to train future statesmen of America. His law curriculum at the College of William and Mary clearly accomplished that goal. Future Chief Justice of the U. S. Supreme Court John Marshall, twenty-seven years old and fresh from the Continental Army, studied law under George Wythe for about six weeks—the only formal legal training Marshall ever received.

Jurist

When the constitution of the Commonwealth of Virginia was amended in 1777, the highest court was designated as the Chancery Court. George Wythe was appointed as justice of the Chancery Court. Wythe served in that capacity until 1788. In one landmark case argued before Wythe's court by Edmund Pendleton, Wythe saw the key issue as one of whether the General Assembly could pardon prisoners in a treason case. Pendleton argued for the execution of the prisoners because the legislature had split on whether or not to grant them pardons. Wythe ruled that the constitution gave the power of pardon to the governor and the legislature had overstepped its bounds in voting on granting pardons. In his summation of the issues in the case, he invoked the principle of judicial review. Wythe said, "Nay more, if the whole legislature, an event to be deprecated, should attempt to over-leap the bounds, prescribed to them by the people, I, in administering the public justice of the country, will meet the united powers, at my seat in this tribunal; and pointing to the constitution, will say to them here is the limit of your authority; and hither shall you go, but no further."

In 1788, the Virginia legislature created a Court of Appeals consisting of five justices. This body became the highest-level court in the commonwealth, putting it in a position to review decisions by the Chancery Court. Wythe chose to remain as the sole judge in the Chancery Court in 1789, taking the title Chancellor of Virginia. His old rival, Edmund Pendleton received an appointment to the new Court of Appeals. This would result in no end of anguish for Wythe as he saw over the next six years 150 chancery cases appealed to the new Court of Appeals. Pendleton and the Court of Appeals, much to Wythe's irritation, overturned a number of his decisions. Indeed, he became so incensed that he wrote and paid for the publication of a book in 1795 taking issue with the Appeals Court rulings.

One case, at least, must have given him satisfaction. In *Page v. Pendleton & Lyons*, in 1793 Wythe upheld the proposition that Virginians must pay, in full, debts owed British creditors before the war. Wythe received considerable criticism from those who wanted to avoid paying debts they had incurred with British firms. However, he considered that common law and decency mandated that the people should pay their just debts. Pendleton and Lyons had argued that the debts were no longer valid. The new Court of Appeals overturned the Chancery Court decision much to Pendleton's glee. However, in 1796, the U. S. Supreme Court ruled that Wythe's decision was correct.

Wythe was a dedicated jurist who would serve as Chancellor for ten years—his career ended by death, not disfavor. One of his last cases allowed him to express his true feelings about slavery. (He had freed his own slaves at *Chesterville* and in Williamsburg.) In *Hudgins v. Wright*, Hudgins intended to send descendents of an Indian out of Virginia. The descendents argued that they were not slaves, but entitled to freedom based on their Indian ancestry. In his opinion in 1806, Wythe wrote, "freedom is the birthright of every human being..." His opinion came well ahead of its time.

Leaving Williamsburg

Once the Virginia government moved to Richmond, Williamsburg became less exciting for George Wythe. By 1789, he had reached an impasse with the administration of the College of William and Mary, and on September 15th, he resigned his professorship at the college. The cause of the dispute is unknown, but he continued to take young men into his home as private students.

In his Williamsburg home, his household consisted of Wythe, one or more students, his housekeeper, Lydia Broadnax, who had been his slave before he freed her, and several other servants. Wythe taught his students Greek, Latin, French, Spanish, English Literature, and Arithmetic. One of his students at that time, Littleton Waller Tazewell, twelve years old, lived with Wythe since his father had moved the rest of the family to his estate called *Kingsmill*. Young Tazewell would grow up to be a distinguished U. S. Senator and Virginia Governor, another example of Wythe achieving his goal of preparing young men for statesmanship.

When Wythe resigned from the college, he took in a young man named William Munford who could not afford to pay tuition. Wythe taught him in his home at no charge. He even acquired scientific equipment to teach Munford physics. Munford would later write about this time in Wythe's life. His mentor had become more introverted after his wife's death and his resignation from the college. He would walk down the Duke of Gloucester Street in Williamsburg and not notice people or speak to them when they spoke to him. Wythe had always been aloof, but he had also always been cordial to the people around him. Townspeople could tell that something was bothering Chancellor Wythe. However, his physical health must have been fine. Munford wrote of one incident in which he and Wythe walked five miles from his house in the city to visit the Taliaferros at *Powhatan*. Wythe was deep in thought and unresponsive to Munford's conversation, but clearly, he was in good physical condition if he was able to walk that distance at age sixty-six.

By 1791, Wythe decided to leave Williamsburg and move to Richmond. He missed the bustle of government activity; and the long journey to the new capital four times a year to attend to the Chancery Court duties had become a nuisance. There was little left in Williamsburg to hold him. He had lost his wife; he no longer had an association with the college, and the important affairs of government were no longer there. But Wythe would not abandon William Munford; he invited the young man to come to Richmond and continue to live as his guest and student. Lydia and the other household staff packed Wythe's belongings, including his treasured books and scientific equipment, loaded them into his coach and wagons, and made the long trip to Richmond in September 1791 with Wythe and Munford.

Lydia, William, and the others, except for Wythe, must have been shocked by what they saw as they arrived at Richmond. The capital at that time was a rough assemblage of wooden buildings scattered along the shores of the James River. There were scarcely any brick buildings or grand avenues. They moved into a wooden frame house on top of Shockoe Hill—a house at the southeast corner of 5th and Grace Street, formerly owned by William Nelson. The small yellow house faced the river. Wythe could walk from his house to his Chancery Court chambers in the basement of the capitol. He took advantage of his free time to continue his studies of ancient Hebrew with local Rabbi Isaac Seixas, and he had a laboratory set up in his home where he and William Munford performed electrical experiments. For the next fifteen years, George Wythe would become a welcome and frequent visitor in the homes of Richmond dignitaries and would continue to instruct young men in his chambers or as private students in his home.

In 1800, Wythe represented Virginia in the Electoral College balloting for president. A tied vote in the Electoral College sent the decision to the House of Representatives. His good friend Thomas Jefferson emerged as the winner after lengthy balloting, defeating incumbent John Adams. Again, in 1804, Wythe represented Virginia and cast his ballot for Jefferson in the Electoral College. This time Jefferson easily defeated challenger Charles Cotesworth Pinckney and won his second term.

During the last few years of his life, George Wythe had two young men in his household. One was a young former slave, Michael Brown, referred to as a mulatto. Wythe taught Michael to read and write and then began his education in Latin, Greek and science. Wythe's actions would have received condemnation by most of Richmond's residents. The second young man living with Wythe was his great-nephew, the grandson of Wythe's sister, Anne. George Wythe Sweeney shared his great uncle's name, but not his character. He was a profligate teenager who spent his time gambling and carousing around Richmond. Perhaps George Wythe hoped to reform his great-nephew.

In 1803, Wythe made a will leaving bequests to Lydia, Michael, and another former slave. In this will, the bulk of Wythe's estate went to George Wythe Sweeney. Three years later, Wythe wrote a codicil to his will directing that Michael be raised by Thomas Jefferson. Wythe provided that Jefferson would have access to his Bank of Virginia stock income to support and continue Michael's education. It is clear from this action that Wythe had great affection for Michael. He made no such guardianship provision for Sweeney.

By this time, Wythe was aware that Sweeney had been stealing from him. The boy had taken some of Wythe's books and, possibly, a terrestrial globe intended for Thomas Jefferson, and sold them on the street in Richmond. Wythe wrote a second codicil three weeks after the first. In that document he directed that his Bank of Virginia stock be divided with half going to Michael and the other half going to Sweeney.

One day, Lydia caught Sweeney going through Wythe's desk. Sweeney found blank checks in his great uncle's desk; he also found Wythe's will and codicils. He learned from those documents that he would come into a sizeable estate when his great-uncle died; but that he would have to share it with a freed slave apparently was too much to bear for young Sweeney.

In April of 1806, he presented a check at the Bank of Virginia payable to himself and bearing a forged George Wythe signature. Sweeney followed this forgery with five or six more, and the bank manager turned the evidence over to the sheriff. On May 25th, George Wythe rose as usual, went to the well and drew a bucket of water, poured the water in the cistern of his shower, and then stood under the spout as the bracing cold water poured over him. He had performed this ritual for most of his eighty years. After dressing, he went into his study and began reading his paper. Lydia, attuned to the rhythm of her former master's day, began preparing his usual breakfast of eggs, toast, and coffee.

As Lydia began frying the eggs, Sweeney entered the kitchen. She offered to cook breakfast for him. He said he would just have toast and coffee as he was in a hurry to go somewhere. While Lydia's back was turned, Sweeney poured himself a cup of coffee from the pot and apparently added a yellow powder to the pot. When Lydia turned, she saw Sweeney throw a scrap of paper into the fire. Sweeney quickly ate his toast, drank his coffee, and left the house.

Lydia carried Wythe his breakfast, and then she and Michael had theirs in the kitchen as they usually did. Within a short time, Michael was gravely ill. He had excruciating abdominal cramps, nausea, and vomited repeatedly. Soon, Lydia experienced the same symptoms and, in her agony, discovered that George Wythe was similarly affected. Fortunately, a doctor lived next door and he came immediately. There was little he could do.

Perhaps because she had only taken a small sip of coffee, Lydia recovered and continued to care for Michael and Wythe. On his sick bed, Wythe examined checks delivered by a bank messenger and confirmed that they were forgeries. While Lydia attended to Wythe and Michael, the sheriff arrested George Wythe Sweeney on a charge of forgery and took him into custody. On June 1, Michael Brown died. An autopsy found signs of poisoning.

When Wythe heard of Michael's death he said, "I shall not be far behind." He called for his friend Edmund Randolph and dictated another codicil to his will. He clearly suspected that his great-nephew had poisoned him and murdered Michael. In the codicil, he revoked all bequests to Sweeney and left his estate to Sweeney's siblings. After signing the codicil, he said, "It is not my desire that this unfortunate nephew of mine shall be prosecuted or punished, further than this codicil will punish him, for the offences which he stands charged. I dread such a stigma being cast upon my name or my sister's." The charge Wythe referred to at that time was forgery. The authorities had not yet charged Sweeney with murder. Wythe, anticipating that his death was inevitable, requested that they autopsy his body as well. He also asked his friends to search Sweeney's room. They did so and discovered evidence of arsenic there.

On June 5th, Wythe said, "I am murdered." On Sunday, June 6th, he said, "Let me die righteous." Then he died.

George Wythe Sweeney eventually stood trial for the murder of his great-uncle. Lydia Broadnax could provide the most damning evidence. She had seen him reading Wythe's will, and she knew that no one else could have poisoned the coffee. She said, "I didn't see him, but it looks monstrous strange." Yellow arsenic powder was discovered in Sweeney's room and on his person. But the jury took only a few minutes to return a verdict of not guilty. The local newspaper, *The Enquirer*, reported that the strongest evidence, the testimony of the "negroes," was not admitted, thus leaving the prosecution with a weak case. The charges of forgery also failed to stick on appeal—Sweeney never stood trial for the murder of Michael Brown. Sweeney moved west, a free but impoverished man.

**Memorial Tablet to George Wythe
at St. John's Churchyard, Richmond**

When news of George Wythe's death reached the citizens of Richmond, church bells rang throughout the city. An Anglican and a Presbyterian minister had attended him as he died. Before burial at St. John's Church, his body lay in state in the House of Delegates. *The Enquirer* issue of June 10, 1806 wrote, "Kings may require mausoleums to consecrate their memory, saints may claim the privilege of canonization; but the venerable George Wythe needs no other monument than the services rendered to his country, and the universal sorrow that country sheds over his grave."

George Wythe

Thus ended an eighty-year life of avid intellectual curiosity, decorum, and dedication to the highest principles of justice and service to others. George Wythe had greatly surpassed his ancestors in longevity, prosperity, and, most importantly, in public service. He had no children of his own, but he nurtured, guided and educated numerous young men, many of whom went on to distinguished public careers of their own, serving their country as President of the United States, U. S. Senator, and Chief Justice of the Supreme Court.

George Wythe's legacy also includes his mark on the constitution of the Commonwealth of Virginia and the U. S. Constitution. He bravely inscribed his name on the founding document of the new republic, *The Declaration of Independence*, testifying to his patriotism. As America's first law professor, George Wythe created the model for instruction still used in law schools today. He personally established a standard for the practice of law that none have surpassed and few have equaled in the last 250 years.

Profiles in Colonial History

Profiles in Colonial History

Peyton Randolph
First Father of Our Country

Chapter 6
Peyton Randolph
First Father of Our Country

It was the Spring of 1754. Much had changed in London during the fifteen years since Peyton Randolph had entered the Middle Temple as an eighteen-year-old law student. Now his native Virginia was on a collision course with the mother country. The royal governor of Virginia had unilaterally imposed a tax—he called it a fee—on landowners seeking his signature on land grants, and Randolph, representing the Virginia House of Burgesses, was in London to redress this wrong.

Randolph was confident in his ability to seek a resolution of this disagreement from the Privy Council. He felt sure that his good name and his conviction that the governor had overstepped the bounds of the English constitution would persuade the courtiers that the so-called pistole fee should be discontinued.

Two years earlier, in April 1752, Lt. Governor Robert Dinwiddie, recently arrived in Virginia, had started off on a bad note with the House of Burgesses by refusing to sign ten laws passed by the House; he reported that those laws had been vetoed by the King in the Privy Council. (Although the crown could overturn laws enacted by colonial legislatures, that royal prerogative was seldom exercised.) Dinwiddie's refusal came as a shock since the laws had been on the books in Virginia for three years and had been acted upon. Vetoing those laws posed serious legal and administrative problems in the colony. But the bigger issue, the House of Burgesses found, was the idea that the Privy Council would meddle in laws that were only of local interest. The British central government had not done so to that extent before, and the House of Burgesses saw the veto by the Privy Council as a violation of their rights as the elected representatives of the citizens of Virginia to make laws for the <u>internal</u> regulation of the colony.

Dinwiddie followed the veto announcement with his decision to charge a fee of one pistole (about£1 then, $240 today) for each land grant that required his signature. A backlog of 2,700 land grants awaited his signature to gain legal status. In an attempt to eliminate Dinwiddie's fee, the House of Burgesses dispatched Peyton Randolph, a member of the House for only six years, to London to petition the Privy Council to overturn the Lt. Governor's pistole fee, arguing that only the Burgesses could impose taxes on citizens of the colony. They believed that the Lt. Governor had violated the constitutional rights of all Virginians.

This assignment from the House of Burgesses put Peyton Randolph in an awkward position: as the King's Attorney General, he had a responsibility to support the Lt. Governor and his council; but he also believed that the Burgesses' position regarding the pistole fee was correct. When Dinwiddie heard that the House of Burgesses had resolved to send Randolph to England, he prorogued (discontinued without dissolving) the

Peyton Randolph as a Young Attorney

General Assembly. And when Randolph actually left for England, he dismissed him as Attorney General, accusing him of abandoning his post, and appointed George Wythe to take Randolph's place as the King's Attorney.

In England, Randolph learned that the mood within the court and Parliament had begun to shift against the colonies; the prevailing view was that the colonists would have to accept that the powers in London could and would legislate for them, or they would suffer the consequences. Dinwiddie's pistole fee was an early sign of the growing constitutional crisis that would lead inexorably to American independence.

Peyton Randolph also learned that those colonials who had the nerve to oppose London's control could expect harsh treatment. In his case, when the issue came before the Privy Council, they accused him of accepting a bribe—the House of Burgesses had appropriated £2,500 to pay his expenses and compensate him for arguing their case in London. In addition, the Privy Council warned the Virginia House of Burgesses that if they paid the money to Randolph, they would be guilty of misappropriation of the Crown's revenues.

In the end, Randolph returned to Virginia with a partial victory. On the one hand, the Privy Council ordered that Dinwiddie could collect the fee only on land grants east of the Allegheny Mountains, and ordered that the governor sign the 2,700 backlogged land grants without the fee. On the other hand—and far more importantly—the Privy Council had challenged the right of the House of Burgesses to appropriate local revenues _and_ denied the Burgesses' exclusive right to levy taxes. The Privy Council's decision regarding the levying of taxes preceded the colonial revolt over _taxation without representation_ by one decade.

When Peyton Randolph returned to the House of Burgesses, they praised him for skillfully handling the pistole fee issue, but he cautioned the House that the real issue—the House's prerogative over local legislation—was not settled. In fact, that right to self-government had just experienced the first of what would be a series of intolerable incursions by the central government in London.

Beginnings

Peyton Randolph came from perhaps the most influential and most widely respected of Virginia families. His grandfather, William, called "Councilor Randolph," immigrated to Virginia from Warwickshire, England in 1651. He and his wife, Mary Isham Randolph, settled at *Turkey Island* on a bend in the James River near modern-day Richmond. There they raised thirteen children.

Peyton's father, John, their fifth son, had also made trips to London on behalf of Virginia. In 1728, he had gone to London for the College of William and Mary to secure funds for the Indian School Library. In 1732, he had gone back to London to represent the House of Burgesses, presenting an argument for an excise tax on tobacco to be paid by importers in Great Britain.

Sir Robert Walpole, British Prime Minister, noticed how skillfully John Randolph dealt with the government, and he arranged for that patrician colonial to receive a knighthood. John returned to Virginia as Sir John Randolph.

Sir John served as clerk of the House of Burgesses (a position later held by George Wythe). The faculty of the College of William and Mary elected Sir John Randolph to his first term in the House of Burgesses in 1734. Soon after, he was unanimously elected to serve as Speaker of the House and Treasurer. However, his tenure as Speaker and Treasurer was a short one; he died in March 1737, leaving a well-endowed trust for the support of his wife, Susannah Beverley Randolph, for the education of his three sons, and for the care of his daughter Mary.

His oldest son, Beverley, lived in Gloucester County, farming and serving as a judge of the county court. Sir John's other sons, Peyton and John, and daughter Mary spent their childhood years in the family home in Williamsburg, the capital of Virginia. Peyton and John followed their father's example, becoming well-respected attorneys and legislators.

Peyton (bearing his maternal grandmother's surname), born in 1721, attended the College of William and Mary, and when he was eighteen, he traveled to London to enter the Inns of Court, spending four years studying English law. He was admitted to the bar in London on February 10, 1743; then he returned to Williamsburg and began his practice of law. His brother, John, following six years behind Peyton, completed his studies of law in London in 1749 and then began his own legal career in Williamsburg.

Peyton Randolph House in Williamsburg, Virginia

Peyton Randolph practiced law primarily before the General Court rather than the lower county courts. He made little attempt to expand his law career beyond that venue, concentrating instead on a career in colonial government. Thomas Jefferson, an admirer of Peyton Randolph, said of him, "...he was well-read in the law; and his opinions, when consulted, were highly regarded,...but generally too a listlessness to go into [the full development of his practice]: for being heavy and inert in body, he was rather too indolent and careless for business, which occasioned him to get a smaller proportion of it at the bar than his abilities would otherwise have commanded." Randolph must have considered his law practice as more of a stepping-stone into a political career and public service, which would dominate his life in later years.

Peyton Randolph married Elizabeth Harrison of *Berkeley* in March 1746. She was the daughter of Colonel Benjamin and Anne Carter Harrison. Elizabeth's brother, also named Benjamin, would be a signer of the Declaration of Independence for Virginia, Speaker of the House of Burgesses, and Governor of the Commonwealth of Virginia. His son would be the ninth President of the United States. Peyton and Elizabeth, whom he called Bess, lived their life together in Peyton's childhood home in Williamsburg.

A Life of Public Service

In 1748, five years after Peyton Randolph was admitted to the bar, Lt. Governor William Gooch appointed him to the position of King's Attorney General. In that capacity, Randolph sat on the Governor's Council, advising them on English law. He also advised the House of Burgesses on legal issues, and he represented the colonial government in civil or criminal cases brought before the General Court.

The citizens of Williamsburg elected Peyton Randolph to represent them in the House of Burgesses in October 1748, carrying on a legislative tradition from his grandfather and father. He soon came under the eye of the most powerful legislator in Virginia, John Robinson, who held the position of Speaker of the House as well as Treasurer of the colony. Randolph presented himself well, dressed stylishly in the fashions of the day, exhibiting the confidence of a high-born Virginian. He was a sedentary man with intellectual curiosity who enjoyed the finer things in life and his appearance showed it. Robinson appointed Randolph to two important standing committees: the Committee of Propositions and Grievances; and the Committee of Privileges and Elections.

Randolph and Lt. Governor Gooch had a very cordial relationship, but soon Gooch had returned to England, and, after a two-year delay, Lt. Governor Robert Dinwiddie arrived in Virginia. Randolph's relationship with Dinwiddie would always be strained, the pistole fee being one of a number of problems that would divide them.

In 1752 at the time of the pistole fee issue, the House of Burgesses declared in a resolution that, "Whoever shall hereafter pay pistole, as a Fee to the Governor, for Use of the Seal to Patents for Lands, shall be deemed a Betrayer of the Rights and Privileges of the People." Randolph may not have drafted that language, but he certainly subscribed to the principle, and he willingly put his career on the line when he "abandoned" his position as King's Attorney General and sailed to England to redress the Lt. Governor's trampling on the rights of the House of Burgesses. Removed from office over the pistole fee matter, Randolph soon returned to the Attorney General position, willingly relinquished by George Wythe, once Lt. Governor Dinwiddie decided that his dismissal had sufficiently humbled Randolph.

In the period between 1752 and 1755, Randolph's stature grew within the House of Burgesses as a representative of the City of Williamsburg and, at other times, the College of William and Mary. He served on three of the five standing committees and was elected to the chairmanship of the Committee of Courts of Justice. A year later, he was chosen to chair the Committee of Privileges and Elections. In November 1762, Randolph became chairman of the Committee of Propositions and Grievances, the committee that served as the legislative filter, determining what issues would be heard by the House of Burgesses—a most prestigious and critically important position as collision with the King and Parliament neared.

A somewhat humorous affair—the Virginia Blues—involving Peyton Randolph and many other leading lights of Virginia society took place in 1755. The French had encroached on Virginia's frontier territories. The previous year, the government had dispatched Colonel George Washington to deal, at first through diplomacy, with the French. When diplomacy failed, military tactics proved no more effective. In June 1755, General Edward Braddock's combined force of British regulars and Virginia militia met defeat at Fort Duquesne.

Frontier settlers now more frequently came under attack by Indians who were taking advantage of the colony's weak military position. The House of Burgesses and the Lt. Governor had to take action. In addition to appropriating funds to support Colonel Washington's militia, a rather ill-conceived additional measure was taken. Thomas Jefferson penned the best description of this situation as he recounted the life of Peyton Randolph in 1816:

After Braddock's defeat on the Monongahela in 1755, the incursions of the Indians on our frontiers spread panic and dismay thro[ugh] the whole country; insomuch that it was scarcely possible to procure men, either as regulars or militia, to go against them. To counteract this terror and to set a good example, a number of the wealthiest individuals in the colony, and of the highest standing in it, in public as well as in their private relations, associated under obligations to furnish each of them two able bodied men, at their own expense, to form themselves into a regiment, under the denomination of the Virginia Blues, to join the colonial force on the frontier, and place themselves under its commander, George Washington, then a Colonel. They appointed William Byrd, a member of the council, Colonel of the regiment, and Peyton Randolph, I think, had also some command. But the original associators had more the will than the power of becoming effective soldiers. Born and bred in the lap of wealth, all the habits of their lives were of ease, indolence and indulgence. Such men were little fitted to sleep under tents, and often without them, to be exposed to all the intemperances of the seasons, to swim rivers, range the woods, climb mountains, wade morasses, to skulk behind trees, and contend as sharp shooters with the savages of the wilderness ….

Fortunately, for these highborn and pampered militiamen, they never saw action. Peyton Randolph and his regiment made it to Winchester where George Washington had his camp, but the French and Indians did not appear. Randolph returned to Williamsburg untested and unscathed.

Francis Fauquier replaced Lt. Governor Dinwiddie in June 1758. News from London made it clear that Parliament was embarking on a course of action that the General Assembly in Virginia needed to monitor closely. Concern over the cost of the French and Indian War in America (an extension of the Seven Years War in Europe) prompted Parliament to consider ways of causing the colonies to bear some of the cost of the war.

In February 1759, the House of Burgesses passed the Agent Act, which called for the engagement of a London-based representative to monitor the situation in the central government and keep the colonial legislators informed. They also created a new standing committee, the Committee of Correspondence, within the General Assembly to give direction to the agent. The Committee of Correspondence had twelve members—four from the Council and eight from the House. Peyton Randolph was one of the House members of this new committee.

The Committee of Correspondence soon took on a coordinating role within the General Assembly, focusing both houses on matters of vital interest, and inevitably, Randolph came into conflict with the Lt. Governor. Over the next few years, Peyton Randolph's chairmanship of the House Committee of Propositions and Grievances and his membership on the Committee of Correspondence gave him extraordinary power over the issues that would become crucial in defining Virginia's role in the coming conflict with King and Parliament.

By 1764, the Committee of Correspondence had learned through their agent, Edward Montague, that Parliament was considering requiring the purchase of stamps in the colonies to be affixed to all legal documents, newspapers, and various other papers. The revenue generated from the sale of the stamps would defray some of the British cost of their military presence in America.

To the members of the House of Burgesses, the Stamp Act was nothing more than a tax, imposed on the colonists without their consent. This proposed tax was even more onerous than the pistole fee in that it was conceived by the Parliament in London, a body in which the colonists insisted they had neither direct contact nor representation.

The Committee of Correspondence wrote to Edward Montague, giving him the impossible assignment of preventing passage of the Stamp Act in Parliament. However, by November 1764, it was clear that Montague could not influence Parliament. Stronger measures would be necessary. The House of Burgesses, with Peyton Randolph presiding over the Committee of the Whole, met to consider what course of action to take to prevent Parliament from abrogating Virginians' rights to self-government, at least with respect to taxation. The House decided to draft an address to the king and "memorials" (petitions) to both houses of Parliament.

The burgesses, at this time, seemed willing to work within the normal channels of central government to defeat the Stamp Act. They appointed a committee of seven men to draft the address and the memorials. According to Thomas Jefferson, Peyton Randolph drafted the address to the king, and George Wythe drafted the memorials for Parliament.

The tone of the language in the address and the memorials was polite, but asserted what the burgesses believed were the constitutional rights of all Englishmen. They wrote that they "… conceive it to be a fundamental principle of the British Constitution, without which freedom can nowhere exist, that the people are not subject to any taxes but such as are laid on them by their own consent or by those who are legally appointed to represent them." They likened Virginians to "mere slaves" if Parliament imposed the Stamp Act taxes upon them.

The Lt. Governor, on reading the text of the burgesses' messages to king and Parliament, said they were "…very warm and indecent." Had warmer members of the house drafted the resolutions, Fauquier would have found them even more indecent, for Randolph had moderated the committee language skillfully to maintain some semblance of respect for the institution of Parliament and the crown.

The Committee of Correspondence immediately dispatched the address and memorials with a letter of instruction to Montague, charging him with the task of presenting them to Parliament and the king. These efforts of the House of Burgesses were disregarded in London, Parliament refusing to even make note of the memorials in their record.

On March 22, 1765, King George gave his approval to the Stamp Act passed by Parliament. The news reached Virginia in May as the General Assembly was beginning their spring term. On May 29, the House of Burgesses met as a committee of the whole with Peyton Randolph presiding. A new member of the house, Patrick Henry inflamed Randolph and other members of the legislature when he proposed five resolutions, reiterating the constitutional rights of Virginians in a more aggressive tone.

Reconstructed Colonial Williamsburg Capitol of 1705

Peyton Randolph took great exception to Henry's incendiary rhetoric, arguing accurately that neither the Parliament nor the king had responded directly to the House of Burgesses' address or memorials. He felt that Henry had presented nothing new and that the hostility of his words would do nothing to bring about a conclusion favorable to Virginians.

Thomas Jefferson, a student at William and Mary at the time, observed the action within the House chamber at the Capitol. He wrote that Randolph strode out of the chamber saying, "By God, I would have given 500 guineas for a single vote." Henry had just won, by a narrow margin, approval of all five of his resolutions.

The Virginia resolutions appeared in the *Virginia Gazette* quickly and soon newspapers in other colonies reprinted them. Lt. Governor Fauquier, infuriated by the resolutions, dismissed the General Assembly. He would keep the House of Burgesses quiet for the next year by proroguing the General Assembly for the fall term of 1765 and the spring term of 1766.

But the Stamp Act incited a strong reaction throughout the American colonies. In October 1765, a "Stamp Act Congress" met in New York. Virginia had no representative at that congress. The attendees prepared a Declaration of Rights with fourteen points (paraphrased below), asserting their rights as Englishmen:

1. Colonists owe allegiance to the crown

2. Colonists are entitled to all the inherent rights and privileges of natural born subjects of Britain

3. No taxes should be imposed on colonists without their personal consent or that of their representatives

4. Colonists are not and cannot be represented in the House of Commons in Britain

5. Colonists' only representatives are those they choose within the colonies, and no taxes have ever been imposed on the colonists except those imposed by their own colonial legislatures

6. All funds given to the crown by colonists are free gifts of the people, and it is unreasonable for Parliament to grant to the crown the property of colonists

7. Trial by jury is an inherent and invaluable right of every British subject in the colonies

8. The Stamp Act is a subversion of the rights of the colonists

9. The duties will be extremely burdensome

10. Profits from the colonies enrich Britain through the goods that colonists purchase from British merchants and manufacturers

11. Trade restrictions recently imposed would make it impossible to purchase British goods

12. Prosperity, happiness, and growth of the colonies depend on full and free enjoyment of the colonists' rights and liberties

13. Colonists have the right to petition Parliament and the crown

14. It is the colonists' duty to petition to the best of their ability for the repeal of the Stamp Act

Although Peyton Randolph had no opportunity to participate in the Stamp Act Congress and its Declaration of Rights, he clearly found it coincident with his own position on the issue of colonial self-governance.

While the Stamp Act Congress met in New York, George Mercer arrived in Williamsburg from England to serve as the stamp distributor for Virginia. An angry mob met him and demanded his immediate resignation. Although Lt. Governor Fauquier rescued Mercer, a day later the beleaguered man proclaimed that he would "… not proceed further with the Act until [he] receive[d] further orders from England and not then until…the assent of the General Assembly of this colony …."

Peyton Randolph found himself in the middle once again: as Attorney General, he had to enforce the law; but as a Virginian and a student of English law, his sympathy lay with the protestors.

The Stamp Act went into effect on November 1, 1765. The next day, the General Court convened for its regularly scheduled session. The Lt. Governor—Chief Justice of the General Court—and his council members attended, as did Attorney General Peyton Randolph. No other attorney from the colony attended court that day. The attorneys stayed away rather than purchase stamps for each of the legal papers they would have filed in court. The Lt. Governor adjourned the General Court until April, taking no other action regarding the boycott of his court. In addition, the Lt. Governor did not press the issue of the Stamp Act during the winter of 1765-1766, much to the relief of Peyton Randolph.

In London during the winter, Parliament reacted to the protests from America by repealing the Stamp Act—but with a catch. They linked the repeal to a Declaratory Act that re-affirmed their right to legislate in all matters for the colonies. The Stamp Act repeal and the Declaratory Act received the king's approval on March 18, 1766.

Parliament had slapped the colonies in the face with their Declaratory Act gauntlet. However, the death of John Robinson, Speaker of the House of Burgesses and Treasurer, delayed the reaction in Virginia. A scandal soon emerged: Robinson had held those two powerful posts for twenty-eight years, and during that time, he had misappropriated a large amount of the colonial treasury for personal business, as well as making loans to some of his closest associates. The total exceeded £100,000 (about $18 million today).

Robinson had named Peyton Randolph as one of three executors of his estate. Randolph wisely resigned that position; in time, as Attorney General, he would sue the Robinson estate for repayment of the treasury funds. Randolph also wanted to succeed Robinson as Speaker of the House and Treasurer. He had worked for that honor for eighteen years and, with Robinson's unexpected death in May 1766, he had his opportunity.

Peyton Randolph, however, would not achieve all of his ambitions. Lt. Governor Fauquier realized that too much power had been vested in Robinson. In fact, a similar scandal had plagued the colony when Sir John Randolph had been in the House of Burgesses. In 1734, John Holloway, the Speaker of the House and Treasurer, had to resign over allegations of mismanagement of colonial funds. Sir John had then ascended to those two positions.

Peyton Randolph's Office in His Williamsburg Home

Fauquier arranged, with approval of the Board of Trade in London, to separate the two positions. From then on, no one could hold both the Speaker of the House and Treasurer positions simultaneously. On May 20, 1766, Fauquier named Robert Carter Nicholas Treasurer of Virginia, subject to the approval of the General Assembly. Nicholas would be approved and serve with distinction; eventually he would serve as a justice in the Chancery Court of the Commonwealth of Virginia.

On November 6, 1766, Archibald Cary nominated Peyton Randolph for Speaker of the House, and Richard Henry Lee nominated Richard Bland for Speaker. Peyton Randolph won the election and would never again have serious competition for the leadership of the legislature in Virginia. Randolph had attained the highest political rank his father had achieved, but events would dictate that he would never be Sir Peyton Randolph. The Colony's separation from England would prevent the bestowal of that social honor.

Upon his election to the speaker's chair, Peyton Randolph resigned from the King's Attorney position; his brother John replaced him in that capacity. Under John Robinson, the power vested in the speaker had grown substantially; nothing happened in the House of Burgesses without Robinson's approval. Peyton Randolph moved to make the House more collegial, more open to debate. He increased the size of the committees and provided opportunities for the newer burgesses to participate in committee affairs. Randolph also worked hard to portray a genuine openness to differing views on the legislative issues. Although he came clearly from the high social strata called, by some, the "squirearchy," Randolph made it clear in the way he presided over the House of Burgesses that legislators from all areas of the colony and all social backgrounds would be respected. His colleagues admired his fairness and openness. His reputation as a moderate, even-handed, and open-minded leader of legislators would spread well beyond Virginia.

Acts of Parliament continued to destabilize the situation in America. In 1764, Parliament had passed the Currency Act that allowed British merchants to refuse to accept colonial currency as payment for debts. British sterling was in short supply in America, and the colonies had substituted their own currency, which had been acceptable prior to the act.

In 1765, Parliament passed the Quartering Act, requiring colonial assemblies to pay for the billeting of British troops in their territory. The act did not, however, force private citizens to provide lodging of troops in their homes—a common misconception. The Currency Act and the Quartering Acts caused renewed resentment of the central government in London in each of the colonies.

Following news of these latest acts of Parliament, the Massachusetts Bay legislature passed a non-importation agreement and distributed a copy of their bill to the other colonies as part of a circular letter. They called on each of the colonies to pass similar measures banning importation of British goods. They hoped that British business interests would lobby Parliament to abandon its punitive treatment of the colonies.

Lt. Governor Francis Fauquier died in March 1768. John Blair, the president of the Council, sat as acting governor until a new governor could be appointed. As the House of Burgesses began its spring term, Peyton Randolph had the Massachusetts Bay colony circular letter read to the assembled legislators. Within one week, the House unanimously approved resolutions to send, yet again, a petition to the crown and memorials to the houses of Parliament requesting reversal of Parliament's recent acts directed against the colonies.

Randolph and other moderates in the House feared a repeat of the resolutions drafted by Patrick Henry during the Stamp Act controversy, so Randolph appointed a large committee to draft the petition and memorials. The committee, chaired by Richard Bland, had twelve members (Patrick Henry was not one of them). Surprisingly, this large committee reported its draft to the House in four days; and the House accepted the committee's work a few days later. Randolph's hopes were realized—the language made the case clearly and diplomatically.

The Council (the upper house of the Virginia General Assembly) approved the House of Burgesses' drafts, and John Blair added his concurrence as acting Lt. Governor. The Committee of Correspondence sent the documents to Virginia's London agent for immediate delivery to the crown and Parliament. They also communicated their action to the other colonial assemblies.

A new governor, Norborne Berkeley, Baron Botetourt, arrived in October 1768. He received a warm welcome and took his place in the vacant Governor's Palace. Peyton and Elizabeth Randolph entertained Lord Botetourt in their home only a short walk (or carriage ride) from the Governor's home.

Lord Botetourt attended the ceremonial joint session of the House of Burgesses and Council in May 1769 for his first formal welcome to the General Assembly. Peyton Randolph made these pointed comments in his address to the Governor:

> … [Virginia's] *Burgesses claim … all their ancient rights and privileges, particularly a freedom of speech and debate, exemption from arrest, and protection for their estates, and lastly for* [the Speaker], *that no mistakes of his might be imputed to the House.*

Lord Botetourt diplomatically assured them that he would "… take care to defend them in all of their just rights and privileges." Randolph and Botetourt had begun on a conciliatory note, but their cordiality could not endure the events that would soon pit the American colonies against the mother country.

In England, Parliament remained unmoved by the latest memorials, and embarked on an even harsher course, imposing embargoes on New England ports. Colonists now faced arrest and transportation to London to stand trial where they would have no support for their defense.

News from London in the spring of 1769 could not have encouraged Randolph. Charles Townshend, Chancellor of the Exchequer, had proposed a series of new taxes and duties on goods imported into the colonies. Some of the goods affected were glass, lead, paint, paper, and tea.

The Virginia House of Burgesses soon tackled these planned encroachments on colonial rights. Randolph, in his capacity as Chairman of the Committee of Correspondence, had been in contact with the speakers in the other colonial assemblies. He had that correspondence entered into the House record.

On May 16, 1769, the House met to consider the state of the colony and to discuss what Randolph had learned from his counterparts in the other colonies as well as from the Virginia agent in London. Their meeting took place in secret. Following their consideration of the intelligence, the House passed four resolutions without debate. These resolutions restated Virginians' basic constitutional rights as Englishmen: the sole taxing authority for Virginians was the House of Burgesses; they had the right to petition directly to their sovereign to redress wrongs; and transporting colonial citizens out of their colony to stand trial "is highly derogatory to the rights of British subjects."

Randolph communicated these Virginia resolutions to the other colonial assemblies via the Committees of Correspondence. The resolutions also appeared in the *Virginia Gazette* on May 18, 1769. In that same issue, the newspaper reported that Governor Botetourt, having learned of the four resolutions, sent his clerk, Nathaniel Walthoe, to summon the burgesses to his council chamber. When Peyton Randolph led the burgesses into the Council Chamber, the only man present was the governor. Without preamble, the governor said, "Mr. Speaker, and gentlemen of the House of Burgesses: I have heard your resolves and augur ill of their effect; you have made it my duty to dissolve you; and you are dissolved accordingly." The House of Burgesses was thus disbanded on May 17, 1769.

The burgesses marched out of the capitol behind Peyton Randolph and followed him up Duke of Gloucester Street and into Anthony Hays' Raleigh Tavern. The publican made the Apollo Room available to them to meet and decide their next course of action. They elected Peyton Randolph as their "moderator" and then considered what action they could take to further protest Parliament's actions. Following Massachusetts' lead, they adopted a similar plan to boycott all British goods coming into Virginia.

The next day, Randolph presided over the meeting of the former burgesses as they considered a series of formal statements that asserted their loyalty to the crown but protested the Townshend duties, and pledged to boycott British goods until the Townshend duties were removed. They called themselves "associators," and the first to sign the articles of association was Peyton Randolph. Now Randolph had reached the point of no return—he realized that the time for conciliation had passed. Parliament's punitive approach to the colonies would have to be met by strong resolve among all of the colonies acting in unison.

In spite of colonial protests, the Townshend Acts became law on June 29, 1769. Colonial legislative assemblies had had enough; they began to communicate openly with their counterparts in other colonies and began to think about another joint response to the abuse they perceived coming from the British government.

Later in the summer, Randolph traveled to New York. He was an appointed member of a royal commission to resolve a boundary dispute between New York and New Jersey. The commission meetings in New York gave him an opportunity to sample public opinion there with regard to the acts of Parliament. On his way to New York, he stopped in Philadelphia and met with people there to get their opinions as well.

While Randolph was in New York, Governor Botetourt ordered the General Assembly back in session. In Randolph's absence, the people of Williamsburg elected him to be their representative in the forthcoming legislative session. By September 28, 1769, Randolph had returned to Williamsburg.

Botetourt anticipated that Parliament would repeal the Townshend Acts and hoped that would resolve the growing tension in the colonies. The governor failed to appreciate the depth of the budding Americans' concern over Parliament's incursions into areas of colonial constitutional rights—self-government, putting it simply. Parliament would not concede that individual colonial legislatures should be the sole enactors of their own internal regulations and the exclusive taxing authorities within the colonies; colonial assemblies would not yield their traditionally held authority to an aggressive central government in London.

The General Assembly convened on November 7, 1769. This session in Virginia would focus primarily on internal issues such as the tobacco economy and Indian relations. The burgesses felt cordial toward the royal governor and held a Christmas ball in his honor. But the burgesses' wives came to the ball in gowns made of homespun Virginian fabric rather than their usual imported British fashions, making the point that the boycott of British goods had not been breached and would not be as long as the Townshend duties remained in effect.

During the spring session of the Virginia General Assembly, word arrived that British soldiers had fired on a crowd of citizens in Boston—the Boston Massacre of March 5, 1770. The Virginia legislators also learned that Parliament had repealed the Townshend duties, as predicted by Lord Botetourt; but Parliament had retained the duty on tea, showing that they still maintained their prerogative to impose taxes on the American colonies. The constitutional issue clearly had not been resolved. These events led to a renewed agreement to boycott British goods, signed by Randolph and the other associators on June 22, 1770.

Williamsburg remained quiet over the sultry summer of 1770. Governor Botetourt died suddenly in October. His replacement would not share Lord Botetourt's cordiality toward the Virginians. John Murray, Fourth Earl of Dunmore, received his appointment as Royal Governor of Virginia in July 1771.

For the next two years, Randolph maintained contact with his counterparts in the other colonial assemblies and attempted to ensure that an effective boycott of British goods continued within Virginia. This period also saw Randolph involved in a number of local civic projects. He served on the

Board of Visitors of the College of William and Mary and participated in the planning for a hospital in Williamsburg.

In March 1773, Randolph became embroiled in what should have been a minor issue—the prosecution of currency counterfeiters who had produced counterfeit £5 notes that destabilized Virginia's currency. After their arrest in Pittsylvania County, Governor Dunmore had them transported to Williamsburg where they were interrogated, tried for their crime, and sentenced to be held in the Williamsburg jail.

Some burgesses argued that Dunmore had violated the counterfeiters' rights by having them removed from the county where the crime was committed and tried in another jurisdiction—a parallel to the larger concern of British transportation of colonial defendants to England to stand trial.

The House of Burgesses drafted an address to the governor containing these words:

The duty we owe our constituents obliges us, my Lord, to be as attentive to the safety of the innocents as we are desirous of punishing the guilty; and we apprehend that a doubtful construction and various execution of the criminal law does greatly endanger the safety of innocent men.

This was followed on March 12, 1773, with a request by Dabney Carr of Louisa County for the Committee of Correspondence to maintain formal contact with other colonial legislatures. The driving issue was the threatened transfer of people from the colonies to England to stand trial. The revitalized committee was established with Peyton Randolph as chairman and with ten other members, including Thomas Jefferson, Patrick Henry and Richard Henry Lee.

The Committee of Correspondence met on March 13. They appointed John Tazewell of Williamsburg to be their clerk. Peyton Randolph, Robert Carter Nicholas, and Dudley Diggs were named as a select committee to act for the whole committee when it might be impractical to call them all to Williamsburg.

These committees of correspondence in the various colonies came to annoy the royal governors, who viewed direct communication between legislatures in the colonies as a threat to their own authority and control. Royal Governor Hutchinson of Massachusetts said that the committees of correspondence were a "glaring attempt to alter the constitution of the colonies, by assuming to one branch of the legislature the powers of the whole....It was an act which ought to have been considered an avowal of independency, because it could be justified only upon principles of independence."

In September, the Virginia Committee of Correspondence learned that Parliament had encouraged the East India Company to ship tea to America to force the issue of payment of the duty. Randolph viewed this as an intentionally provocative act by Parliament. He expected it would lead to a confrontation when the ship bearing the tea arrived in an American port. How right he was. On December 16, 1773, *HMS Beaver* and *HMS Eleanour*, docked in Boston harbor with a cargo of East India Company tea, served as the stage for a dramatic demonstration. Colonists disguised as Indians boarded the vessels and emptied the ships' holds of tea, dumping the cakes of tea into the harbor. Parliament would react sternly to this audacious act in the Massachusetts Bay colony—the infamous "Boston Tea Party."

By May 1774, the British government's reaction was known in Virginia. Parliament had passed the Boston Port Act, which became law on March 31, 1774. The Act made it unlawful to discharge, lade or ship goods, wares, or merchandise into or out of Boston until such time as the British Treasury and the East India Company received compensation for the loss of the duties payable to the crown and payment for the destruction of the tea. To enforce this embargo, Britain sent regular troops—Redcoats—under General Thomas Gage to seal off the port and patrol the city.

In Virginia, Randolph talked to individual burgesses privately and got their agreement to hold off this most volatile topic until the House finished with their more mundane but pressing business. He knew that when they took up this intolerable act by Parliament, no other business would be possible and the governor would likely dissolve the General Assembly.

Finally, with routine business finished, during the evening of May 23, 1774, Patrick Henry, Thomas Jefferson, Richard Henry Lee, Francis Lightfoot Lee, and George Mason drafted a resolution of protest against Parliament's punishment of Boston. They presented their resolution to the House of Burgesses the next day. In retrospect, it appears rather mild: they called for a day of fasting and prayer on June 1 in sympathy for the people of Boston whose rights were being denied.

However, Governor Dunmore did not view the resolution as mild. As soon as he learned of it, he dismissed the legislators, dissolving the General Assembly on May 26. Peyton Randolph led his colleagues yet again to the Raleigh Tavern, where they resurrected the Virginia Association, pledging to refrain from purchasing any goods from the British East India Company except saltpeter and spices. But, more importantly, they charged the Committee of Correspondence—now operating independently of the General Assembly—to call for a "general congress" among all of the American colonies. The purpose of the congress would be "to deliberate on those general measures which the united interests of America may from time to time require." Clearly, by this time in Virginia, the concept of America united against Britain had emerged full born.

On May 28, the Committee of Correspondence sent appropriate letters to each of the colonies calling for a general congress, resulting in the First Continental Congress, which would meet in the Fall of 1774. On May 29, Randolph learned that at a town meeting held in Boston two weeks before, people of Massachusetts Bay had called on all colonies to join them in rejecting <u>all imports</u> from Britain and her West Indian ports.

Randolph summoned as many former burgesses as he could to return to Williamsburg. On May 30, at the Raleigh Tavern, they agreed to expand their former ban on East India Company goods to all British goods, putting Virginia in harmony with their allies in Boston. Randolph, realizing that they were only a small group, had them agree to hold another conference, scheduled for August 1 in Williamsburg, so that more of the former burgesses could attend and support the boycott agreement. To arrange the conference, Randolph wrote to his absent colleagues, "Things seem to be hurrying to an alarming crisis and demand the speedy united counsel of all those who have regard for the common cause." While waiting for the August meeting, the select committee notified the other colonies of the action Virginia had taken so far.

Bruton Parish Church, Williamsburg, Virginia

On June 1, Peyton Randolph, portly and slow of gait, led a procession of burgesses and townspeople to Bruton Parish Church to hear Reverend Price inaugurate the day of fasting and prayer for the citizens of Boston. Sentiments from other parts of Virginia filtered into Williamsburg during the summer. Randolph learned that people in various parts of Virginia were advocating open rebellion against Britain. Such sentiments raised the stakes substantially for the August conference of former legislators that Randolph had arranged.

Building a New Nation

Virginia's circular letter to the other colonies had called for the First Continental Congress. As the former Virginia burgesses assembled in Williamsburg in August to consider the boycott of British goods, they also had to determine who would represent Virginia in the Congress scheduled to convene in Philadelphia in one month.

On August 6, 1774, the convention in Williamsburg approved resolutions establishing an expanded Virginia Association, halting import of all British goods into Virginia, effective November 1, 1774. Importantly, they did not ban the export of Virginia goods to Britain—that would have been economically crippling, as the annual tobacco crop would soon be ready for shipment.

Then the delegates unanimously elected Peyton Randolph to lead the Virginia representatives to the Continental Congress. The other representatives from Virginia were: George Washington, Patrick Henry, Richard Henry Lee, Edmund Pendleton, Benjamin Harrison, and Richard Bland.

By this time, Peyton Randolph believed that only a united front by all of the colonies would restore the rights of the American colonies. But he still wore the mantle of moderation, particularly in contrast to more inflamed advocates of separation among the Virginia delegation—Patrick Henry being the most notable and vocal among them. Randolph arrived in Philadelphia with the reputation of being a cool-headed, dispassionate leader who would allow careful consideration of all viewpoints as he worked for a consensus.

Randolph quickly came to the forefront as the delegates from all the colonies assembled in Carpenters' Hall in Philadelphia. On September 5, the delegates unanimously chose the somber, patrician delegate from Virginia to be the first President of the First Continental Congress. Randolph's steady hand was soon needed, for when they turned their attention to selecting rules of order for their meetings, tempers flared over how votes would be cast: some wanted each colony to have one vote; others wanted colonies to have numbers of votes proportional to the population or the wealth of the colony. Randolph brought the crisis to a close by persuading the delegates that each colonial delegation should cast one vote.

Carpenters' Hall, Philadelphia, Pennsylvania

Silas Deane, a delegate from Connecticut, wrote this characterization of Randolph: "Our President seems designed by nature for this business...he commands respect and esteem by his very aspect, independent of the high character he sustains." Randolph divided the fifty-five delegates in Congress into two committees: one to examine how American rights had been violated; one to consider how Parliament's acts affected American trade and manufacturing.

Randolph met informally with each of the delegates and soon knew that there was a clear consensus on how to proceed. Throughout September, he guided the delegates through their sessions with cool, deliberate, effective leadership, allowing all viewpoints time for consideration.

On September 22, the Congress declared that all imports from Great Britain would be suspended until they could find an appropriate way to ensure American liberty. On September 28, they dealt with a plan of union, a confederation of all the colonies in opposition to British abuses of the colonies. On September 30, Congressional delegates agreed to stop all exports from America to Great Britain effective September 1775. The one-year delay would minimize the hardship on colonies such as Virginia, whose tobacco crop represented its major economic resource.

Two weeks later, Congress approved a Declaration of Rights and Grievances to send to the British government as well as to disseminate within the American colonies. That document carefully articulated once again the complaints individual colonies had previously submitted to Parliament and the crown.

On October 23, Peyton Randolph handed the gavel to Henry Middleton, delegate from South Carolina, and left Philadelphia to return to Williamsburg, the major business of this First Continental Congress being accomplished. Three days later the Congress agreed to meet again in May 1775, and then adjourned.

Randolph returned from Philadelphia in time to attend the expected fall session of the Virginia General Assembly. When he arrived in Williamsburg, he learned that Governor Dunmore was away, leading a military expedition against the Indians on the western frontier. The General Assembly would be delayed because of the governor's absence.

During the winter, when Parliament and the crown responded with hostility to the Declaration of Rights and Grievances, Peyton Randolph knew that he could not wait for Dunmore to convene the House of Burgesses. Action was needed now. He placed a notice in the *Virginia Gazette* for each of the counties to hold elections to choose delegates for a proposed Virginia Convention in Richmond, to begin on March 20, 1775. His notice first appeared on January 19, 1775, and he signed the notice, "Peyton Randolph, Moderator." If Governor Dunmore wanted to find the instigator of rebellion in Virginia, he need look no farther than his neighbor around the corner, Peyton Randolph. Randolph had assumed the leadership position, and he presumably had no intention of backing down.

Randolph had grasped the authority from the governor. He had called for election of delegates—the prerogative of the royal governor to call for elections. This alone could have resulted in Randolph's name being inked on the governor's black list. From Randolph's perspective, he felt it vital that the representatives in the Virginia Convention have the clear authority to speak for their various county constituents. He anticipated that they were about to take critical steps on the path to revolution, steps that must have the support of the majority of Virginians through their freely elected representatives.

Randolph chose to meet in St. John's Church in Richmond to ensure that the Convention would not be disturbed by the governor. On March 20, every county and voting district was represented except for the College of William and Mary. Peyton's brother John was the college's representative, and his loyalty to the crown was without question. He would not take part in what he considered a treasonous convention.

The convention delegates elected Peyton Randolph their president. In his opening remarks, he made it clear that he viewed this convention as taking the place of the legislative session that Governor Dunmore had failed to convene.

Although Dunmore eventually did convene the General Assembly, it was to no avail. From March 20, 1775, onward, the old order was no more. Royal control had failed, and the citizens of Virginia under Peyton Randolph and later leaders would never again submit to royal legislation.

This Virginia Convention is famed for Patrick Henry's spirited call to arms. His address to the convention made it clear that he felt the time for conciliation was over. He noted the hostilities already taking place in Massachusetts and exhorted his fellow delegates to take the necessary steps to form a militia for the defense of Virginia. The delegates accepted Henry's position, and he was given the chairmanship of a committee to determine how to form the militia and arm the colony. On another timely matter, the delegates chose their representatives to the Second Continental Congress. Once again Randolph would lead the delegation.

This time, however, the delegation included the addition of Randolph's first cousin, Thomas Jefferson, as his alternate in case Randolph's health prevented him from attending the congress. Randolph was showing signs that his high-pressure responsibilities and life of overindulgence had taken their toll. He may have been in the early stages of heart failure. He was obese, slow of movement, with swollen legs, and was asthmatic.

The next month, back in Williamsburg, marines from the British schooner *Magdalen*, under cover of night, removed the gunpowder from the city magazine. Dunmore had ordered it taken, he said, for safekeeping. The outraged citizens planned to storm the Governor's Palace, but Randolph persuaded them that if they did so, Dunmore would bring in British troops and place the city under martial law.

Randolph and city leaders called a "Common Hall" or town meeting. They agreed that storming the palace would do no good, and they renewed their demand on the governor to return their gunpowder to the magazine. There the matter rested until word of Dunmore's action spread to other locales. Outrage led to the mobilization of the county militias, with the threat to march on Williamsburg and confront the governor. Hearing this, the governor assembled troops at Yorktown, close enough to respond to his aid in Williamsburg, if needed.

Dunmore summoned Peyton Randolph to the Governor's Palace for a private meeting. Randolph came away from that meeting believing that the governor would back down and return the gunpowder if the threatened militia did not come to Williamsburg. On that basis, Randolph wrote to the commander of the militia in Fredericksburg, "[Dunmore]...will not be compelled to what we have abundant reason to believe he would cheerfully do if left to himself." The next day Randolph left Williamsburg for Philadelphia, believing that the gunpowder crisis had been resolved. Unbeknownst to him, Patrick Henry was marching to Williamsburg at the head of his own militia. In the ensuing standoff, Henry forced the governor to pay £330 (about $60,000 today) for the stolen gunpowder, and then retired without firing a shot.

On his way by coach to Philadelphia, Randolph and his wife learned of the shots fired at Lexington and Concord—the beginning of open warfare between Britain and the American colonies. By the time the delegates convened in Philadelphia, they knew that the government in London would continue to counter their demands with a buildup of British troops.

Randolph again easily won the presidency of the Continental Congress. He knew that congress would have to take more decisive action. However, having served for only two weeks as president, Randolph turned the leadership over to John Hancock of Massachusetts so that he could return to Williamsburg. Governor Dunmore had called the General Assembly into session beginning on June 1, 1775.

When Peyton Randolph arrived in Williamsburg on May 30, city leaders feared for his safety. His name was on a list of men the British government planned to arrest, transport to

England, try, and hang. The small troop of city militia surrounded him and escorted him safely to his home. In their greeting, they called Peyton Randolph "the father of your country," an epithet applied in later years to George Washington.

When the House of Burgesses convened in the Capitol, they elected Peyton Randolph their Speaker. Whatever Lord Dunmore expected to come from calling the burgesses into session, the outcome could not have pleased him. They appointed a committee to examine the powder magazine incident and passed a resolution approving the actions of the First Continental Congress.

On June 8, Dunmore and his family fled the city, boarding British warship *HMS Fowey* at Yorktown. He wrote to the House of Burgesses from the ship:

> *Being now fully persuaded that my person, and those of my family likewise, are in constant danger of falling sacrifices to the blind and unmeasurable fury which has so unaccountably seized the minds and understanding of great numbers of the people, and apprehending that at length some of them may work themselves up to that pitch of daringness and atrociousness as to fall upon me, in the defenceless state in which they know I am in the city of Williamsburg, and perpetrate acts that would plunge this country into the most horrid calamities, and render the breach with the mother country irreparable, I have thought it prudent for myself, and serviceable for the country, that I remove to a place of safety; conformable to which, I have fixed my residence, for the present, on board his Majesty's ship the Fowey, lying at York.*

Within the month, Lady Dunmore and her family transferred to *HMS Magdalen* and set sail for London.

On June 24, 1775, the House of Burgesses adjourned for the final time as a royal colonial legislature. Two days later, Peyton Randolph published a notice in the newspapers calling for delegates to a second Virginia Convention in Richmond, scheduled for July 17, 1775. He signed the notice, "Peyton Randolph, President." By this time, however, he was physically exhausted. The political crisis and his poor health had sapped his limited strength.

When the delegates convened in Richmond, Randolph arranged for them to meet as a committee of the whole with Richard Bland serving as moderator. Bland, eleven years older than Randolph, was also in poor physical condition. The delegates had great concern over the well-being of both of these leaders. In less than a month, Robert Carter Nicholas had diplomatically stepped in and replaced Bland, and on August 16, Peyton Randolph was retired as president so that he could prepare for returning to the Continental Congress. Accompanied by his wife, Randolph went to his home in Williamsburg where he rested for one week.

A Family Divided

During the previous summer of 1774, the Randolph family had publicly split over the conflict with Great Britain. King's Attorney General John Randolph, a protégé of Lord Dunmore, published *Considerations on the Present State of Virginia*, a pamphlet printed in Williamsburg on the same press that produced the *Virginia Gazette*. In this document, John Randolph set himself apart from his brother and other "patriots" placing himself on a lofty, aristocratic pedestal. His pamphlet, laden with hauteur, began as follows:

> *My Address is to the Publick .... When I mention the Publick, I mean to include only the rational Part of it. The ignorant Vulgar are as unfit to judge of the Modes, as they are unable to manage the Reins, of government.... The author of this little Performance was born, and educated in* Virginia. *He was nurtured in the mixed Principles of Obedience and Freedom, as they stand in the* English Constitution. *He has ever held in Contempt the Applause of a giddy Multitude, but the good Opinion of the Wise and Virtuous he has at all Times endeavoured to cultivate.*

Although he published the pamphlet anonymously, there was no doubt in Williamsburg that John Randolph was the author. One can almost hear him sneering at Patrick Henry— one of the "ignorant vulgar," at least in the Attorney

General's mind. He continued in this lengthy pamphlet to outline what he saw as a substantive difference in the Stamp Act (in his view an unconstitutional attempt by Parliament to impose an <u>internal</u> tax on the colonies) and the Tea Duty (a legal exercise of Parliament's right to control trade and an <u>external</u> tax, in his opinion). However, he clearly was out of touch with the feelings of the vast majority of Virginians, and not only the "vulgar" but also the high-born members of society.

In the pamphlet, John Randolph also departed from the theoretical and denigrated the day of fasting and prayer held the month before his publication by the burgesses and leaders of Williamsburg—most notably, his brother Peyton. Robert Carter Nicholas wrote an even longer response to John Randolph's pamphlet, saying with regard to his denigration of the day of fasting and prayer, "Upon this subject [Randolph] seems to have opened every vein of Paltry Ridicule."

John Randolph predicted that chaos would reign throughout America if the colonies were to win their independence from Britain. He went on to defend Parliament's imposing of punitive measures on the people of Boston. He felt the entire city deserved to have their port closed and British regulars enforcing martial law in their city because of the lawless disposal of the East India Company's tea by a small band of patriots.

The summer of 1774 had to have been a very trying time for the two Randolph brothers and their children. Edmund, John's son, made it clear that his sympathy lay with the American patriots, particularly his uncle Peyton. John's wife, Ariana, and his daughters Susannah and Ariana, remained loyal to him. Within a year, John and his family would abandon Virginia, leaving only Edmund behind.

Death Too Soon

In 1775, with his stamina somewhat restored after the crisis with the governor and the Second Virginia Convention in Richmond, Peyton and Bess Randolph left Williamsburg on August 27, and made the long overland journey once again to Philadelphia. While Randolph had been in Virginia, the Continental Congress had secretly authorized the formation of a standing army, the Continental Army, under command of General George Washington. John Randolph's son Edmund served General Washington as his Aide de Camp, much to his father's displeasure.

The Second Continental Congress reconvened after a short recess on September 5, and Peyton Randolph was there. However, too few delegates attended to reach a quorum until September 13, at which time John Hancock refused to relinquish the presidency to Peyton Randolph, much to the surprise of the other delegates. On September 22, Randolph took his seat in a committee to develop foreign trade—a critical issue since trade with Britain had been suspended. The most vital trade goods would be war materials.

Peyton and Bess Randolph shared a house in Philadelphia with Thomas Jefferson, Thomas Nelson, Jr., and some other delegates. On the evening of October 22, 1775, the Randolphs and Thomas Jefferson dined outside the city at the home of Mr. Hills. After dinner, Randolph began to choke and had an apparent stroke. Jefferson called it "an apoplectic fit." By eight p.m., Peyton Randolph was dead.

His body lay in state in Philadelphia at his lodgings; his funeral service took place at Christ's Church, attended by the delegates to the Continental Congress. Edmund Randolph arrived in Philadelphia, on leave from General Washington's camp, to escort Elizabeth Randolph back to Williamsburg. His uncle's body lay temporarily in the Francis family vault. Eventually, his remains were brought back to Williamsburg and interred in a vault under the Wren Chapel at the College of William and Mary.

In 1784, John "The Tory" Randolph died in England. At his request, his remains were returned to Virginia and lie alongside his brother's body in the crypt beneath the Wren Chapel. Their father's remains lie beside them. Those two brothers, divided by the American Revolution, now repose together under the chapel of the college they both attended, served and loved. Peyton Randolph's will left his estate to his wife, then his brother John and nephew Edmund. Peyton and Bess Randolph had no children. His estate was appraised at £12,980 (about $2.5 million today) and included 100 slaves.

**The Wren Building at The College of William and Mary in Virginia
The chapel wing is on the right.**

Peyton Randolph came slowly to the recognition that independence from Great Britain was the only way to preserve colonial Americans' rights. He arrived at that decision through reason, knowledge of English law, and with the realization that diplomatic and conciliatory approaches toward the central government in London had failed numerous times.

Thomas Jefferson, who had observed Peyton Randolph as Speaker of the House of Burgesses, Moderator of the Virginia Conventions, and President of the Continental Congress, said this of his cousin:

> *He was indeed a most excellent man; and none was ever more beloved and respected by his friends. Somewhat cold and coy towards*

strangers, but of the sweetest affability when ripened into acquaintance. Of Attic pleasantry in conversation always good-humored and conciliatory, with a sound and logical head,...[as King's Attorney General] *he aimed at a candid and just state of the transaction, believing it more a duty to save an innocent than to convict a guilty man.*

The Wren Chapel contains no memorial marker for Peyton Randolph, the first father of our country, the first president of our congress, the leader of the American independence movement. Visitors may not enter the Wren Chapel crypt, but if they could, they would find there three dusty stone vaults containing the remains of the reunited Randolph family.

Peyton Randolph's memorial must therefore be the existence of the United States of America, a nation that he did not live to see, in a form of government that he might not have anticipated, but a testament to his belief in the people's inherent right to self-government—a fitting memorial to a man who placed his well-being, honor and integrity at risk in the quest for the rights of Americans.

Image Credits

Cover Image *Colonial Williamsburg in Fall,* photograph by author.

Page 1 overleaf, Images 5 and 6 from *Das sechste Theil Americae oder Der Historien Hieron. Benzo das dritte Buch. Darinnen erzehlet wirk, wie die Spanier die...,* published in Oppenheim, 1620. The Kraus Collection of Sir Francis Drake, Library of Congress. <u>Note:</u> sketch of what Harriot may have looked like added by author.

p. 2, *Harriot and an Indian with a lens, starting a fire,* drawing by A. Loker.

p. 7, Detail from *Map of London,* ca. 1570, in author's collection.

p. 10, A portion of images 5 and 6 from *Das sechste Theil Americae oder Der Historien Hieron. Benzo das dritte Buch. Darinnen erzehlet wirk, wie die Spanier die...,* published in Oppenheim, 1620. The Kraus Collection of Sir Francis Drake, Library of Congress.

p. 15, Illustration of Back-staff and Cross-staff by author.

p. 18, *Syon House*, photograph by author.

p. 34, *George Calvert, 1ˢᵗ Lord Baltimore,* by Gerard Soest, courtesy of the Enoch Pratt Free Library, Central Library/State Library Resource Center, Baltimore, Md.

p. 37, detail from image above.

p. 40, *Cecil Calvert, 2nd Lord Baltimore,* by Daniel Mytens, the Elder. The Enoch Pratt Free Library, Central Library/State Library Resource Center, Baltimore, Md.

p. 50, *Margaret Brent (ca. 1601-1671),* Conjectural painting by Louis Glanzman, Maryland State Archives, MSA SC 1545-0789, April 11, 2006.

p. 52, *Larke Stoke Manor,* photograph by author.

p. 76, *Patrick Henry before the Virginia House of Burgesses,* by Peter F. Rothermel in 1851. Red Hill, Patrick Henry National Memorial, Brookneal, Virginia.

P. 84, *Ralegh Tavern,* photograph by author.

P. 88, *St. John's Church, Richmond,* photograph by author.

P. 90, *Powder Magazine, Williamsburg,* photograph by author.

P. 97, *Patrick Henry,* portrait cropped from engraving by E. Wellmore after painting by J. B. Longacre and miniature in possession of John S. Fleming of Virginia. Prints and Photographs Collections, Library of Congress, reproduction number LC-USZ62-7668.

p. 100, *George Wythe,* image number 148-CD-13-9. The U. S. National Archives and Records Administration.

P. 104, *Reconstructed Colonial Williamsburg Capitol of 1705,* photograph by author.

P. 108, *George Wythe's Home in Williamsburg on the Palace Green,* photograph by author.

P. 110, *Colonial Williamsburg Courthouse,* photograph by author.

P. 120, *The Wren Building, College of William and Mary*, photograph by author.

P. 129, *Memorial Tablet to George Wythe*, photograph by author.

p. 132, *Peyton Randolph*, by Charles Wilson Peale. Independence National Historical Park, Philadelphia, Pennsylvania.

P. 134, *Peyton Randolph as a Young Attorney*, portrait by C. W. Peale, National Archives.

P. 137, *Peyton Randolph House in Williamsburg, Virginia*, photograph by author.

P. 143, *Reconstructed Colonial Williamsburg Capitol of 1705*, photograph by author.

P. 147, *Peyton Randolph's Office in His Williamsburg Home*, photograph by author.

P. 157, *Bruton Parish Church, Williamsburg, Virginia*, photograph by author.

P. 159, *Carpenters' Hall, Philadelphia, Pennsylvania*, image number HABS PA, 51-PHILA.229-4, Library of Congress, Prints and Photographs Division, Historic American Buildings Survey.

P. 168, *The Wren Building of The College of William and Mary in Virginia*, photograph by author.

CPSIA information can be obtained at www.ICGtesting.com
Printed in the USA
BVOW02s1538200514

353592BV00001B/2/P

9 781928 874164